C# and VB.NET Conversion
Pocket Reference

Jose Mojica

Beijing · Cambridge · Farnham · Köln · Sebastopol · Tokyo

C# and VB.NET Conversion Pocket Reference

by Jose Mojica

Copyright © 2002 O'Reilly Media, Inc. All rights reserved.
Printed in the United States of America.

Published by O'Reilly Media, Inc., 1005 Gravenstein Highway North, Sebastopol, CA 95472.

Editor:	Ron Petrusha
Production Editor:	Jane Ellin
Cover Designer:	Emma Colby
Interior Designer:	David Futato

Printing History:

April 2002:	First Edition

ISBN: 978-0-596-00319-7
[LSI]   [2011-04-29]

Contents

C# & VB.NET Conversion Pocket Reference

Introduction

If you are anything like me, the following is a common scenario: You are writing some code not in the language you traditionally use. Although you know a needed command in your language of choice, the keyword in the language you are using is not even remotely similar, and you can't even think of a word to type in the help file to try to get it. You want to be able to flip through a short book that has your keyword in it, along with the equivalent way of coding it in the new language you are using. This book attempts to fill that need.

This book—as well as my recognition of the need for it—grew out of my own experience. I was teaching courses on VB.NET exclusively. Then one day, I was asked to teach a C# course. It was in front of about 25 C# students that I figured out, the hard way, that knowing VB.NET does not mean you automatically know C# (and I even knew C++).

Microsoft has advertised that the .NET runtime is language agnostic, and that C# and VB.NET are so close that switching between the two is really nothing more than choosing between semicolons and Dims. That is true to a certain extent. However, during that week in front of the firing squad, I discovered that there were a lot of differences between the two, some really obvious, and some more subtle.

The differences, it seemed to me, occur in three main areas: syntax, object-oriented principles, and the Visual Studio

.NET IDE. *Syntax* concerns the statements and language elements; you say tomato, I say toe-mah-toe. *Object-oriented* differences are more subtle, and concern differences in implementation and feature sets between the two languages. They concern things such as inheritance and method overloading. *IDE* differences include things like compiler settings, which are attributes you set through the IDE that have different effects depending on what language you use. There is also a fourth area of difference: *language features* that are present in one language but have no equivalent in the other. These unique language features are also covered in this book.

After my C# class was over, I began writing a book to help me switch between the two languages. I realized that a lot of people were in the same boat, because we find an example in the docs or in a book that does not have the other language's equivalent, or because we are in a job that requires the use of the other language, or because we are curious about what the other language can do, or most commonly because we would like to be able to tell people, "I know both."

Before I begin, some ground rules. Neither language is better than the other. You will not hear me say, "VB is better than C#," or vice versa. I love both languages equally. Also, this book assumes you know one of the two languages, but does not make an assumption about the one you know. The information is presented in a language-neutral point of view so that programmers from each camp can read a section and feel that it is targeted to them.

Conventions Used in This Book

Italic is used for filenames, URLs, and to introduce new terms.

`Constant width` is used for code and to indicate keywords, parameters, attributes, and other code items within text.

`Constant width bold` is used to highlight parts of code sections.

| VB | This icon indicates a Visual Basic .NET code fragment. |

| C# | This icon indicates a C# code fragment. |

Syntax Differences

Syntax differences are the most common differences that we think about when comparing two languages. Syntax differences refer to differences in the keywords and format of statements used to perform identical tasks. For instance, in C#, a language statement is terminated with a semicolon; in VB, a language statement is terminated with the carriage return/linefeed character sequence. In this section, we'll survey the syntactical differences between VB.NET and C#.

Case Sensitivity

One major difference between the languages is that C# is case sensitive, while VB.NET is not. That means that while it is okay in VB.NET to write:

```
system.console.writeline("hello world")
```

(all in lowercase), in C# that line results in an error. The correct way to invoke this command in C# is:

```
System.Console.WriteLine("hello world");
```

Both C# and VB.NET compile to a language known as *Intermediate Language* (IL). Interestingly, IL is case sensitive, which means that VB must convert lines at compile time to match the correct casing of the original command at the IL level.

A side effect of not being case sensitive is that at times, the compiler may not match casing correctly to the original declaration of a function, resulting in incorrect behavior. For example:

| VB |
```
Class Account
    Overloads Function toString( _
        ByVal Format As String) As String
```

```
        Return "My String with Format"
    End Function

    Overloads Overrides Function toString( ) As String
        Return "My String"
    End Function
End Class

Module App
    Sub Main( )
        Dim acct As Object = New Account( )
        System.Console.WriteLine(acct.ToString( ))
    End Sub
End Module
```

This code has strange results in VB.NET. The VB compiler
cases the toString method incorrectly to match the first definition of toString in the Account class (with lowercase T),
rather than matching both definitions to the one inherited
from System.Object (with capital T). The end result is that
toString does not override the ToString method in the base
class, and the toString method is never called. This example
shows the complexity of having a case-insensitive language in
a case-sensitive world.

What happens if you add two public functions in C# with
the same name but cased differently? VB cannot use the function, and complains that it cannot resolve the function. For
example, a Banking class written in C# has a MakeDeposit
and a makedeposit method. You can reference the DLL in
VB, and you can create an instance of the Banking class, but
if you try to use either MakeDeposit or makedeposit, the
compiler complains that it cannot figure out which one to
use. To prevent this, you could ask the compiler to test for
Common Language Specification (CLS) compliance. The
CLS describes what is legal to make public in order to be
compatible with other languages. To tell the compiler to
check for CLS compliance, add the following line of code to
the *AssemblyInfo.cs* file in your C# project:

```
[assembly: System.CLSCompliant(true)]
```

If you're using the C# command-line compiler, simply add the line to your source code file after any using statements. After adding that line, the C# compiler gives you an error if two public functions in your class differ only by case.

Line Termination

C# statements can be split into multiple lines with CRLF and are terminated with a semicolon. VB.NET lines can only be broken with a continuation character and are terminated with CRLF. The following code illustrates breaking up lines in C#:

```
//one line of code in C#
string sName = sFirstName +
               sLastName;
//semicolon signals the end of a statement
```

The semicolon indicates the end of a code statement. You can break up the line in almost any place. You can go as far as putting each word on a separate line and even adding comments to the end of each segment. For example:

```
string
sName //variable
= //operator
sFirstName //first name
+ //plus operator
sLastName;
//semicolon signals the end of a statement
```

You can do the same with string literals if you precede the string with the @ symbol:

```
string
sName = @"John Jacob Jingle
Hymer Smith";
```

However, be aware that code like that above results in a string with a carriage return embedded.

In VB, to break a line into segments, you must add a space and the underscore character. For example:

```
VB    'one line in VB
      Dim sName As String = sFirstName + _
               sLastName
```

As in C#, you can break up every word if you like, as in the example below. (However, unlike C#, in VB it is illegal to put comments after each segment.)

```
VB    'one line in VB
      Dim _
      sName _
      As _
      String _
      = _
      sFirstName _
      + _
      sLastName
```

Unlike C#, it is illegal to break up string literals into two separate lines.

Comments

C# distinguishes between single line comments and block comments. Single line comments use a double slash, as follows:

```
C#    //This is a comment
      void MakeDeposit(int Amount)
      {
          int _Balance; //stores the Account balance
```

Notice that there is a comment above the function declaration and a comment after the declaration of the _Balance field. When you use the double slash, all text after the slashes is assumed to be part of the comment. A block comment uses a slash followed by an asterisk (/*) at the beginning of the block, and an asterisk followed by a slash at the end of the comment block (*/). Here's an example:

```
C#    /*
      Function: MakeDeposit
      Scope: Public
      Description: Increases the balance for the account.
      Author: Jose Mojica
```

```
    */
    public void MakeDeposit(int Amount /*Deposit Amount*/, int
    AmountAvail /*how much is available*/)
    {
    }
```

Block comments enable you to write full paragraphs of comments without having to put double slashes on every line, but they also allow you to insert a comment within a single line of code. Block comments can have comments embedded within them, as in the following:

[C#]
```
    /*
    //this is an embedded comment
    */
```

VB.NET has only a single-line comment. Comments are made either with the Rem statement or with a single apostrophe (the preferred method). Here are some examples:

[VB]
```
    'This is a comment
    Rem This is another comment
    Sub MakeDeposit(ByVal Amount As Integer)
        Dim _Balance As Integer 'Account balance
    End Sub
```

One limitation with comments in VB is that you cannot insert a comment in the middle of a line of code, as you can with block comments in C#.

Namespace Declaration and Usage

A *namespace* is a group of classes that have the same name prefix. For example, if the WidgetsUSA namespace has classes named Checking and Savings, the full name for these classes is WidgetsUSA.Checking and WidgetsUSA.Savings. The namespace declaration prefixes each class name within it.

Both VB.NET and C# enable you to define a namespace. Here are some code examples:

[C#]
```
    namespace WidgetsUSA
    {
        namespace Banking
```

```
    {
        public class Checking
        {
        }
        public class Savings
        {
        }
    }
}
```

The same code can be written in VB as follows:

```
Namespace WidgetsUSA
    Namespace Banking
        Class Checking
        End Class
        Class Savings
        End Class
    End Namespace
End Namespace
```

The full names for the classes in these examples are Widgets-USA.Banking.Checking and WidgetsUSA.Banking.Savings. The namespace declarations attempt to make the class names unique for a particular company. However, it gets cumbersome to type long class names in declarations. Therefore, each language provides a statement that allows you to omit the namespace name and use the short class name in declarations instead. In C#, this is done with the using statement:

```
using WidgetsUSA.Banking;
class App
{
    static void Main()
    {
        Checking check = new Checking();
    }
}
```

The equivalent of using in VB is Imports:

```
Imports WidgetsUSA.Banking
Class App
    Shared Sub Main()
        Dim check As Checking = New Checking()
    End Sub
End Class
```

In both C# and VB.NET, you can assign a prefix to a namespace. This helps solve problems of ambiguity in which multiple namespaces have the same class name. Consider two classes: MyCompany.SharedCode.DatabaseClasses.Connection and SomeOtherCompany.Modem.Connection. Suppose a developer writes code to use or import the namespace for each class as follows:

```VB
Imports MyCompany.SharedCode.DatabaseClasses
Imports SomeOtherCompany.Modem

Class App
    Shared Sub Main( )
        Dim cn As Connection
    End Sub
End Class
```

The compiler complains that `Connection` in these declarations is ambiguous; it could be from either namespace. One solution is to assign a prefix to one or both of the namespaces as follows:

```C#
using db=MyCompany.SharedCode.DatabaseClasses;
using SomeOtherCompany.Modem;

class App
{
    static void Main( )
    {
        db.Connection cn;
    }
}
```

Here is the equivalent code in VB.NET:

```VB
Imports db=MyCompany.SharedCode.DatabaseClasses
Imports SomeOtherCompany.Modem

Class App
    Shared Sub Main( )
        Dim cn As db.Connection
    End Sub
End Class
```

The first using statement in C# and the first `Imports` statement in VB assign a prefix (db) to the MyCompany.Shared-Code.DatabaseClasses namespace. You can then use db in your code instead of the namespace name. This is easier to type and also solves ambiguity problems. Of course, you could just use the fully qualified namespace name whenever you refer to the class to solve ambiguity problems.

VB has one enhancement that C# lacks. It lets you use `Imports` not only with a namespace name (as does C#), but also with a class name. For example:

`VB`
```
Imports Microsoft.VisualBasic.ControlChars

Module App
    Sub Main( )
        Dim s As String = "Hello" + NewLine + "World"
        System.Console.WriteLine(s)
    End Sub
End Module
```

The `Imports` statement references a namespace (Microsoft.VisualBasic) and a class (ControlChars). Therefore the code in Main can use the constants in the class without having to use the class' complete name. One of these constants is `NewLine`, which represents a carriage return and a line feed character.

Variable Declaration

In C#, the variable type always precedes the variable name. Here are some examples:

`C#`
```
int x;
decimal y;
rectangle z;
object obj;
```

In VB, the variable name always is first, then the variable type. VB also requires a `Dim` or an access modifier (Public, Private, Friend, Protected, or Protected Friend). A

---

declaration that uses Dim is Private by default. The following VB code is equivalent to the previous C# code:

```
VB    Dim x As Integer
      Dim y As Decimal
      Dim z As Rectangle
      Dim obj As Object
```

Both languages enable you to create an instance of a class using the new keyword. Here are some examples in C#:

```
C#    class Account
      {
      }

      class App
      {
         static void Main( )
         {
            //example 1
            Account acct = new Account( );

            //example 2
            Account acct2;
            acct2 = new Account( );
         }
      }
```

You can combine the object declaration and instantiation onto one line, or you can separate the instantiation from the declaration.

VB has three ways of using the new operator, as illustrated below:

```
VB    Class Account
      End Class

      Class App
         Shared Sub Main( )
            'example 1
            Dim acct As Account = new Account( )

            'example 2
            Dim acct2 As Account
            acct2 = new Account( )
```

```
        'example 3
        Dim acct3 As New Account
    End Sub
End Class
```

All three examples generate the same IL. Example 3 is similar to example 1—it Dims a variable of type Account and creates an object of type Account. Unlike previous versions of VB, example 3 creates an instance of the Account object immediately. In VB 6 and before, when you used the As New notation, the object would not be instantiated until you used it.

Variable Initialization

C# requires you to initialize local variables explicitly. Consider the following declaration:

```csharp
class Account
{
    int Balance;        //instance field

    public void MakeDeposit()
    {
        int tempBalance;    //local variable
        //compiler error
        Console.WriteLine(tempBalance);
    }
}
```

The Account class has a field, Balance, a method, MakeDeposit, and a local variable, tempBalance. In C#, you do not have to initialize fields before using them. Fields are auto-initialized to 0 if they are numeric or to null if they are reference types. However, the C# compiler issues an error if you attempt to use a local variable before assigning it a value.

This is not the case in VB. VB.NET automatically initializes all local variables to 0 or to Nothing (or the equivalent, depending on the class). Consider the following VB code:

```vb
Class Account
    Dim Balance As Integer
```

```
    Sub MakeDeposit( )
        Dim tempBalance As Integer
        'no compiler error
        System.Console.WriteLine(tempBalance)
    End Sub
End Class
```

In this example, both Balance and tempBalance are initialized to 0.

Inside the IL

When both compilers generate the IL for the local variables
in a procedure, they add the init keyword to the variable
declarations section, which tells the JIT compiler to initialize
local variables to 0 or null. This IL code shows the use of the
init keyword:

```
.locals init ([0] int32 tempBalance)
```

The C# compiler enforces the rule that local variables be initialized at compile time.

Declaring Function Parameters

There are three kinds of parameter direction: in (or by
value), in,out (or by reference), and out. When an argument
is passed by value, changes made in the called function are
not reflected back to the caller; when an argument is passed
by reference, they are reflected. With reference parameters,
memory is allocated by the caller but the function can change
the value. With out parameters, the memory is allocated and
the value set by the function, with the caller receiving only
the value. Both C# and VB can use all three forms of parameters; however, they work a little differently between the languages. Consider the following two examples in C#:

```
void MakeDeposit(int x, ref int y, out int z)
{
```

```
    x = 10; //changes not reflected to caller
    y = 10; //changes reflected to caller
    z = 10; //required. Changes expected and
            //reflected to the caller.
}

void MakeDeposit(object obj1, ref object obj2,
                 out object obj3)
{
    obj1 = new object(); //changes not reflected
                         //to caller.
    obj2 = new object(); //changes reflected to
                         //caller, which now has a
                         //reference to a different
                         //object than the
                         //original one
    obj3 = new object(); //required. Function
                         // must allocate
                         //the object.
}
```

The first example accepts value types, and the second example accepts reference types. Both versions are shown to illustrate what it means to send an object by reference. Sometimes, developers incorrectly assume that if you pass in an object by value to a function, the function cannot change the fields of that object. That is not the case; consider the following code:

```
class person
{
    public int Age;
}

class App
{
    static void ChangeAge(person p1)
    {
        p1.Age=10;
    }
}
```

In this example, p1 is a by value parameter, yet if the function changes the Age field, the caller will see that the Age field was in fact changed. "By value" applies only to the object the variable points to; the object's fields can always be changed no matter how the parameter direction was declared. In the case of objects, sending an object by value only means that if the function sets the variable to a different object, the caller will still hold a reference to the original object when the function ends. If an object is sent by reference, and the function sets the variable representing the object to a new object, then the caller will hold a reference to the new object when the function returns.

Out parameters are really reference parameters marked with a special attribute to simplify how parameters are passed when remoting. When the caller and the object live in different machines, the less data that is transmitted in each call across the network, the better. Parameters sent by value only need to be transmitted from the caller to the object and not back. Parameters sent by reference need to be sent twice: from the caller to the object, and then back to the caller. Out parameters only need to be transmitted from the object to the caller.

VB supports all three versions of parameter passing. By value parameters are specified either by omitting a direction keyword as in C# or by using the ByVal keyword:

VB
```
Sub MakeDeposit(ByVal num1 As Integer)
End Sub

Sub MakeDeposit(num1 As Integer)
End Sub
```

The num1 parameter is accepted by value in both routines. You must use the ByRef keyword to pass a parameter by reference, as in the following example:

VB
```
Sub MakeDeposit(ByRef num2 As Integer)
End Sub
```

VB does not have a keyword for out parameters; however, you can apply the <Out> attribute to represent out parameters. For example:

```
Imports System.Runtime.InteropServices
Sub MakeDeposit(<Out( )> ByRef num1 As Integer)
End Sub
```

This code declares the `num1` parameter in MakeDeposit as an out parameter. The C# version is simpler, since the language provides a keyword that automatically adds the attribute. However, placing the attribute in VB accomplishes the same task. A drawback of the VB style is that the language does not enforce the concept automatically. In C#, if you mark a parameter as out, the function must set the parameter to a value before returning to the caller; otherwise, the compiler generates an error. But in VB, you can apply the attribute to a `ByRef` parameter or to a `ByVal` parameter. The latter is a mistake, but the compiler does not enforce the rule.

Passing Function Parameters

In C#, if a function contains `ref` parameters, you must use the `ref` keyword in front of each by reference argument when you call it. The same is true for out parameters—the out keyword must appear before any argument that corresponds to an out parameter. Also in C#, it is illegal to pass in a literal value as an argument for a ref or out parameter. (You cannot pass a number for a `ref int` parameter, for example.) Any variable you pass as a ref argument must be initialized before making the method call. The following code segment illustrates these principles:

```
static void DoSomething(int x, ref int y,
                           out int z)
{
    z=45;
}

static void Main(string[] args)
{
    int y=4; //you must declare a variable
            //and initialize it.
    int z;
    //notice the use of the ref and out
```

```
        //before each ref and out argument.
    DoSomething(5,ref y,out z);
}
```

In VB, you do not use any keywords in front of the method arguments, whether they are ByVal, ByRef, or <Out> ByRef. The example below shows how to call functions with ByRef parameters in VB.NET:

VB
```
Imports System.Runtime.InteropServices

Module Module1
    Sub DoSomething(ByVal x, ByRef y, <Out()> ByRef z)
        z = 45
    End Sub

    Sub Main()
        Dim y As Integer
        Dim z As Integer

        'y and z do not have to be
        'initialized because VB auto
        'initializes variables
        DoSomething(5, y, z)
        'it is also legal in VB.NET to
        'pass literal values for ByRef
        DoSomething(5, 10, 20)
    End Sub
End Module
```

Notice that it is not necessary to use ByRef in front of the ByRef arguments or to initialize argument variables, because VB auto-initializes local variables. Notice too that VB lets you send literal values for ByRef parameters.

Inside the IL

Whenever you make a method call in VB.NET and you use a literal value for a ByRef parameter, at the IL level VB declares a hidden local variable, assigns it the value you are passing, and passes the address of the variable instead of the literal value to the function.

Optional Parameters

In VB, you specify optional parameters as follows:

```vb
Sub MakeDeposit(Optional ByVal x As Integer=10)
End Sub
```

Optional means the parameter may be omitted. In other words, you can call MakeDeposit(20) or MakeDeposit(). If the parameter is omitted, the default value (10 in the declaration for MakeDeposit above) is used. Default values must be constants because if the caller omits the value, the compiler writes a call that uses the default value. Thus, at runtime it appears as though the caller did not omit the value. The ability to omit parameters in the call is specific to the VB compiler. For example, if you write a class in VB with a method that has an optional parameter, and then write code to use the class in C#, your C# code cannot omit the parameter in the call.

You can define a parameter as optional in C# as well using an attribute. However, in C# the parameter will not be optional. If the C# class is used with a VB program, the VB code can omit the optional parameter. In this case, its value will be 0 or nothing, depending on the variable type, since there is no way to specify the default value through attributes in C#. The following code shows how to define a method with an optional parameter in C#:

```csharp
using System.Runtime.InteropServices;
public void MakeDeposit([Optional] int Amount)
{
}
```

Parameter Lists

In C# and VB, you can declare a single parameter as a parameter list (or parameter array)—a parameter that can accept a variable number of arguments, all of the same type, or an array with a variable number of elements. The following code example shows how to define a parameter list array in C# and how to invoke the method that contains it:

```
//definition (meant to be in a class)
public void MakeDeposit(params int[]
                        Amount) { }
//calling the method
//(code meant to be in a function)
Account acct = new Account();
//a call with multiple arguments
acct.MakeDeposit(50,100,20,30);
//a call with no arguments
acct.MakeDeposit();
//a call with an array argument
int[] Amounts = {50,100,20,30};
acct.MakeDeposit(Amounts);
```

The code invokes the MakeDeposit method three times: once with four parameters, once with none, and once with an array. To the .NET runtime, the MakeDeposit call simply accepts an array of integers. If you pass multiple arguments, the compiler generates code to create the array and fill it with the values of the call, then calls MakeDeposit passing this array of values.

The following is the VB equivalent:

```
'definition (meant to be in a class)
Sub MakeDeposit(ParamArray Amount As Integer())
End Sub

'calling the method (meant to be in a function)
Dim acct As New Account
' a call with multiple parameters
acct.MakeDeposit(50,100,20,30)
'a call with no parameters
acct.MakeDeposit()
'here is a call with an array, also acceptable
Dim amts As Integer() = { 100, 200, 30, 50 }
acct.MakeDeposit(amts)
```

Method Declaration

In C#, all methods are functions. Some functions return nothing (void), as in the following:

```C#
public void MakeDeposit(int Amount)
{
}
```

VB distinguishes between two types of methods: Subs and Functions. A Sub is a method that does not return a value. When a VB program is compiled, subroutines are turned into functions that return void, just like in C#. The following code shows a VB.NET subroutine and a VB.NET function:

```VB
Sub MakeDeposit(ByVal Amount As Integer)
End Sub

Function IsOpen(ByVal AcctID As Integer) As Boolean
End Function
```

Notice that in a function you add As after the parameter list, followed by the return type.

Returning Output Parameters

Both C# and VB.NET have a return keyword to return the value of a function and exit the function at the same time. The following illustrates its use:

```C#
public class Person
{
    int m_Age = 10;
    //use of return with a parameter

    public int GetAge()
    {
        return m_Age;
    }

    public void Speak()
    {
        if (m_Age < 1)
            return;
        //do something else here
    }
}
```

The GetAge function returns the contents of the m_Age field; the Speak function returns nothing.

VB has another way to return parameters for compatibility with older versions of VB. You simply set the function name equal to the return value. (Note that doing so does not exit the function automatically.)

Inside the IL

The trick of setting the function name to the output parameter in VB is accomplished at the IL level by declaring a hidden variable with the same name as the name of the function. Because of this, there is a distinction between GetName (the variable) and GetName() (the function). For example:

```
Function GetAge() As Integer
    GetAge = 100
    Return GetAge
End Function

Function GetAge() As Integer
    GetAge = 100
    Return GetAge()
End Function
```

The first version returns 100 to the caller. In the second version, Return GetAge() cause the code to call GetAge infinitely.

VB

```
Public Class Person
    Dim m_Age As Integer = 10

    'use of return with a parameter
    Function GetAge() As Integer
        Return m_Age
    End Function

    Sub Speak()
        If m_Age < 1 Then Return
        'do something else here
    End Sub

    'You can also use the function name
    'to return a value
```

```
    Function GetName( ) As String
        GetName = "Smith"
    End Function
End Class
```

Program Startup

All EXE programs begin with a Main procedure. VB has a feature that also enables a WinForms project to specify a startup form instead of a Main procedure. However, even in this case, programs begin with a Main procedure. (Take a look at "Startup Object" in the "IDE Differences" section to see how this works.)

In C#, Main (with a capital M) is a static procedure in a class. In VB.NET, Main is a shared procedure in a class. In VB.NET, Main can also be inside a Module. (A *module* is a class in which all methods are automatically Shared. See "Classes Versus Modules" later in this section for details.)

Both C# and VB enable you to write a Main procedure in three different ways. In its simplest form, you can write a Main procedure that has no parameters. Here is an example:

[C#]
```
class App
{
    static void Main( )
    {
    }
}
```

[VB]
```
Class App
    Shared Sub Main( )
    End Sub
End Class
```

(Shared in VB.NET is the same as static in C#.) You could also write a Main procedure with an incoming parameter of type string array. This string array contains the command-line arguments used when running the program. For example, a user may run your program as follows:

```
program.exe param1 param2 /param3 "param4 param5"
```

Here is an example of using that form of Main:

```csharp
class App
{
    static void Main(string[] args)
    {
        foreach(string arg in args)
        {
            System.Console.WriteLine(arg);
        }
    }
}
```

```vb
Class App
    Shared Sub Main(ByVal args As String())
        Dim arg As String
        For Each arg In args
            System.Console.WriteLine(arg)
        Next
    End Sub
End Class
```

In this version of Main, args is a string array containing the program's command-line arguments. The command-line arguments do not include the program name; they are the strings that come after the program name. Each argument is separated by a space. To have a string containing a space as a single parameter, you must add quotation marks around it. The code outputs all command-line arguments to the console window. Assuming we were using the command line described earlier, the output is:

```
param1
param2
/param3
param4 param5
```

You can write a third version of Main as a function that returns an integer. This version can take either the string array as a parameter or no parameters. The integer is programmer-defined, which means that you must define meaningful values. Normally, 0 denotes success, and non-zero values denote error conditions. Here is an example:

```csharp
class App
{
    static int Main( )
    {
        return 0;
    }
}
```

```vb
Class App
    Shared Function Main( ) As Integer
        Return 0
    End Function
End Class
```

For backward compatibility, VB also has a Command function that enables you to retrieve the command-line arguments as a single string. Here is an example:

```vb
Imports Microsoft.VisualBasic

Class App
    Shared Sub Main( )
        Dim args As String = Command( )
        System.Console.WriteLine(args)
    End Sub
End Class
```

Exiting Programs/Methods/Loops

VB.NET offers a variety of statements to exit a program, method, or loop. To exit a program, you use the End statement. Placing End anywhere in the code results in the program terminating. For example:

```vb
Module App
    Sub CheckSecurity(ByVal sID As String)
        If sID = "" Then
            End
        End If
    End Sub
    Sub Main( )
        CheckSecurity("")
    End Sub
End Module
```

C# does not have an equivalent method to exit the program. However, both VB and C# can make use of the System.Environment.Exit method. Here is a C# example using the Exit method:

```csharp
class App
{
    static void CheckSecurity(string sID)
    {
        if (sID == "") System.Environment.Exit(1);
    }

    static void Main(string[] Args)
    {
        CheckSecurity("");
    }
}
```

Exit accepts one parameter, the exit code.

VB has several statements for exiting methods, including Exit Sub, Exit Function, and Exit Property. An example with Exit Function is:

```vb
Function MakeDeposit(ByVal Amount As Integer) As Integer
    If Amount < 0 Then
        Exit Function
    End If
    m_Balance += Amount
    Return m_Balance
End Function
```

C# does not have an equivalent method. However, the same task can be accomplished with the return statement. In fact, that's all that VB does internally.

VB.NET also has methods for exiting loops, including Exit Do (for Do-While loops) and Exit For (for For-Next loops). For example:

```vb
Class People
    Dim Total As Integer
    Sub FillAuditorium()
        Dim iCount As Integer
        For iCount = 1 To 500
            Total += iCount
```

```
            If Total > 250 Then
                Exit For
            End If
        Next
        System.Console.WriteLine(iCount)
    End Sub
End Class
```

C# has an equivalent statement, break. The break statement works with for loops, while loops, and switch statements. The following C# code illustrates the use of break to exit a method prematurely:

```
class People
{
    int Total;

    public void FillAuditorium( )
    {
        int iCount;
        for (iCount = 1; iCount <= 500; iCount++)
        {
            Total += iCount;
            if (Total > 250)
                break;
        }
        System.Console.WriteLine(iCount);
    }
}
```

One C# feature not available in VB.NET is the continue statement. The continue statement enables you to advance the loop. The following code demonstrates the use of continue:

```
public class Person
{
    string LastName;
    int Age;

    public static void SearchPeople(Person[] arr, int Age)
    {
        for (int i=0; i < arr.Length; i++)
        {
            if (arr[i].Age != Age)
                continue;
```

```
        System.Console.WriteLine(arr[i].LastName);
      }
    }
  }
```

In this code, the loop in the SearchPeople function iterates an array of Persons looking for any person that matches a specific age. An `if` statement compares a Person's age to the desired age. If they are not equal, the code calls `continue`, which advances the loop and returns to the first line of code in the loop.

Member Scope

When declaring class members such as fields, methods, properties, events, nested classes, etc., C# makes members private by default, while VB makes members (other than fields declared with `Dim`) public by default.

The following table shows the keywords used in each language to denote the scope of a class member:

C#	VB.NET	Comments
public	Public	Default in VB
private	Private	Default in C#
internal	Friend	
protected	Protected	
protected internal	Protected Friend	

Outer classes at the IL level have only two possible scopes: private or public. Private means that the class is available at the assembly level (in most cases this means the project level), and public means that it is visible outside of the assembly. VB.NET uses the `Friend` keyword to denote assembly scope for an outer class. C# uses the `internal` keyword to denote assembly scope.

Static and Shared Methods

Static methods are methods that are not attached to a particular instance of a class. In other words, you may invoke a static method without creating an instance of the class. Along the same lines, a *static field* is a field that is not dependent on the instance of the class. Static fields are allocated when the type (the class in which they are declared) is allocated. Type allocation occurs just before any code that refers to the class executes. Static fields are allocated for the duration of the program.

The limitation of static methods is that they can only invoke other static methods, and they can only use static fields. They cannot call instance methods or use instance fields without first creating an instance of the class. The following code illustrates static methods and fields:

```
class Account
{
    public static int TotalAccounts;
    int m_ID;

    public static int GetNextAccountID( )
    {
        return TotalAccounts;
    }

    public Account( )
    {
        m_ID = GetNextAccountID( );
        TotalAccounts++;
    }
}
```

The Account class contains two fields. One, TotalAccounts, is marked as static. (All fields and functions have been marked as public only for convenience; static fields do not need to be public.) The other, m_ID, is an instance field.

This code also defines a static method called GetNextAccountID. If you study the code, you'll notice that instance functions (such as the class' constructors) can call static functions. Instance functions can also access static fields. It is not legal, however, for a static function to call instance functions or to use instance fields. If a static function needs to call an instance method, it must first create an instance of the type and then call the instance method.

To use static members outside of the class in which they are defined in C#, you must use the class' name. For example, if you would like to access the GetNextAccountID function or the TotalAccounts field, you must do it as follows:

```
class App
{
    static void Main(string[] args)
    {
        int ID = Account.GetNextAccountID();
    }
}
```

It is illegal in C# to invoke a static method or use a static field through an instance variable. For example, the following code results in a compiler error:

```
class App
{
    static void Main(string[] args)
    {
        Account acct = new Account();
        //illegal in C#
        int ID = acct.GetNextAccountID();   //error
    }
}
```

VB also supports static fields and static functions. VB uses the Shared keyword to denote static members. The limitations for shared methods in VB are identical to those in C#. The following code shows the VB equivalent of the previous C# code:

```
Class Account
    Shared TotalAccounts As Integer
    Dim m_ID As Integer

    Shared Function GetNextAccountID() As Integer
```

```
            return TotalAccounts
        End Function

        Sub New()
            m_ID = GetNextAccountID()
            TotalAccounts+=1
        End Sub
    End Class
```

As in C#, VB shared functions can only call other shared methods or use shared fields. It is legal, however, for instance functions to use any shared fields or call any shared methods.

VB enables you to call a shared method or to use a shared field using a variable that points to an instance of the class, as in the following example:

```
VB    Class App
        Shared Sub Main()
            'legal in both languages
            Dim ID As Integer = Account.GetNextAccountID()

            Dim Acct As New Account()
            'legal in VB, not in C#
            ID = Acct.GetNextAccountID()
        End Sub
    End Class
```

As the example shows, it is legal to invoke the GetNextAccountID function using the class name or an instance of the Account class.

Classes Versus Modules

VB.NET supports code modules, which developers use to write libraries of global functions. For example:

```
VB    Module App
        Sub Main()
        End Sub
    End Module
```

The VB compiler translates a module into a class in which all members are marked as Shared (static in C#). The generated class is sealed (NotInheritable). Since every member in a module is Shared, you cannot add instance constructors to the module, only a shared constructor.

There is no equivalent in C#, but a C# developer can simulate a module by writing a sealed class with all methods and fields marked as static. One advantage of using a module over a class with all members marked as static, however, is that in VB you can refer to a member of the module directly without specifying the module's name. Normally when you declare a shared method in a class by hand, you must use the name of the class plus the method to invoke it, as in the following example:

```VB
Class Math
    Shared Function Add(Num1 As Integer, _
                        Num2 As Integer) As Integer
    End Function
End Class

Module App
    Sub Main()
        System.Console.WriteLine(Math.Add(3,4))
    End Sub
End Module
```

To invoke the Add method, you must write Math.Add. In VB, if the method is part of a module, you may omit the module's name:

```VB
Module Math
    Function Add(Num1 As Integer, _
                 Num2 As Integer) As Integer
    End Function
End Module

Module App
    Sub Main()
        System.Console.WriteLine(Add(3,4))
    End Sub
End Module
```

In this case, you need only call the Add method. This is true as long as the compiler can tell what Add method to invoke. If you have two modules that have the same method with the same signature, you must fully qualify the name by adding the name of the module, just as if you were invoking a Shared method from the class.

If you are writing a class in C# to be used in VB.NET and want to make it look like a module, you can simply mark every member in the class as static, then reference the Microsoft.VisualBasic.DLL assembly and add the StandardModule attribute (from the Microsoft.VisualBasic. CompilerServices namespace) to your class, as follows:

```
[Microsoft.VisualBasic.CompilerServices.StandardModule]
public class Math
{
    public static int Add(int num1, int num2)
    {
        return num1+num2;
    }
}
```

A VB project can then refer to the Add function directly without the class name.

If Statements

Both languages have conditional if statements. However, the syntax and semantics differ between the languages. In C#, the conditional statement must be enclosed in parentheses, as follows:

```
if (x > 10)
    DoSomething( );
```

Notice that if is in lowercase, there are parentheses surrounding the conditional statement, and that unlike in VB, there is no need for Then at the end. This example shows an if statement with only one task to perform. If there are multiple tasks to perform, they are enclosed in curly brackets, as follows:

```
if (x < 10)
{
    DoTask1( );
```

```
      DoTask2( );
   }
```

If you want to add an else clause, you use the else keyword in lowercase, as in the following example:

```
C#   if (x < 10)
     {
        DoTask1( );
        DoTask2( );
     }
     else
     {
        DoOtherTask1( );
        DoOtherTask2( );
     }
```

If your else statement needs to test for another condition, it is perfectly fine to include another if statement as part of the else clause, as follows:

```
C#   if (x < 10)
     {
        DoTask1( );
        DoTask2( );
     }
     else if (x > 10)
     {
        DoOtherTask1( );
        DoOtherTask2( );
     }
     else
     {
        DoNothing( );
     }
```

In VB, the syntax is slightly different. VB uses the If and the required Then keywords as follows:

```
VB   If x > 10 Then DoSomething( )
```

There is no need for parentheses around the conditional statement. As in C#, an If statement may perform only one task, or it can perform multiple tasks, as in the following:

```
VB   'when using "End If" the "Then" is optional
     'but VS.NET adds it by default
```

```
If x < 10
    DoTask1( )
    DoTask2( )
End If
```

Instead of surrounding the task block with brackets, VB uses the End If statement at the end of the block. An else clause can be specified with the Else keyword:

```
VB    If x < 10 Then
          DoTask1( )
          DoTask2( )
      Else
          DoOtherTask1( )
          DoOtherTask2( )
      End If
```

In this case, the End If goes after the Else block. If your else must have another If condition, then, unlike C#, you cannot simply write another If in the same line. Instead VB has a special ElseIf keyword that you must use for the second condition, as follows:

```
VB    If x < 10 Then
          DoTask1( )
          DoTask2( )
      ElseIf x > 10 Then
          DoOtherTask1( )
          DoOtherTask2( )
      Else
          DoNothing( )
      End If
```

When combining clauses in an if statement, both languages use different symbols to represent operators. The following table tells you what operators to use in each language:

VB.NET	C#	Operator
And	&&	and
Or	||	or
Not	!	Boolean opposite
=	==	equals
<>	!=	not equal

Short-Circuiting

In addition to syntax differences, if statements in both languages differ in semantics. The main difference is the use of short-circuiting in C# by default. Consider the following example:

```
static bool DoTask1()
{
    return true;
}

static bool DoTask2()
{
    return false;
}

static void Main(string[] args)
{
    //it is unnecessary to execute
    //DoTask2 because DoTask1 returns
    //True, which is enough to satisfy
    //the or clause
    if (DoTask1() || DoTask2())
    {
    }

    //it is unnecessary to execute
    //DoTask1 because DoTask2 returns
    //False, which means the clause is
    //False
    if (DoTask2() && DoTask1())
    {
    }
}
```

In this example, the function DoTask1 always returns true, and the function DoTask2 always returns false. C# uses a technique called *short-circuiting*, which means that if part of the statement makes the entire statement true or false, there is no need to process the rest of the statement. For example, in an or operation, if at least one of the clauses is true, then the entire statement is true. In the example above, DoTask1 returns true; therefore, there is no need to execute DoTask2.

The second half of the code example contains an and operation. In an and operation, all clauses have to be true. If one of
the clauses is false, there is no need to evaluate the rest of the
statement. In this example, DoTask2 returns false; therefore,
there is no need to evaluate DoTask1.

VB does not short-circuit by default. In VB, all parts of the
conditional statement are executed unless you use the special keywords AndAlso or OrElse. For example:

```
VB    Shared Function DoTask1() As Boolean
          Return True
      End Function

      Shared Function DoTask2() As Boolean
          Return False
      End Function

      Shared Sub Main()
          'VB evaluates each portion of the
          'if clause without short-circuiting
          If DoTask1() Or DoTask2()
          End If

          If DoTask2() And DoTask1()
          End If
      End Sub
```

Both the Or clause and the And clause will execute DoTask1
and DoTask2 without short-circuiting. If you would like to
short-circuit, you must replace And with the AndAlso keyword and Or with the OrElse keyword, as follows:

```
VB    Shared Function DoTask1() As Boolean
          Return True
      End Function

      Shared Function DoTask2() As Boolean
          Return False
      End Function

      Shared Sub Main()
          If DoTask1() OrElse DoTask2()
          End If
```

```
    If DoTask2() AndAlso DoTask1()
    End If
End Sub
```

This code uses short-circuiting. In the OrElse statement, only
the DoTask1 clause is executed. In the AndAlso statement,
only the DoTask2 clause is executed.

Inside the IL

If you use And and Or in VB.NET instead of the short-circuiting equivalents, at the IL level VB executes all the functions
involved in the If first, then compares the results. In the case
of short-circuiting, VB executes one statement, then checks
the result to see if it needs to continue. If it does not, it skips
the rest of the statements. Otherwise it executes the second
statement and checks again, and so on.

Conditional Statement

Both C# and VB.NET have a conditional statement that
enables you to test one clause and return one value if the
clause is true and another if the clause is false. In C#, this is
done in the following fashion:

```
static void Main(string[] args)
{
    int Balance = 45;
    int Withdrawal = 50;

    string msg = (Balance < Withdrawal) ?
      "Insufficient Funds" : "Successful";
      msg = (Balance < Withdrawal) ? DoTask1() :
      DoTask2();
}
```

This C# code shows two uses of the conditional statement.
The format for the conditional is:

```
(true/false_clause)  ? value_for_true :
                       value_for_false
```

Notice from the code example that you can return literal values for the true and false portions, or you can invoke functions that return a value.

VB.NET also has a conditional in the form of the IIf function. For example:

```vb
Sub Main( )
    Dim Balance As Integer = 45
    Dim Withdrawal As Integer = 50

    Dim msg As String = IIf(Balance < Withdrawal, _
                        "Insufficient Funds", _
                        "Successful")
    msg = IIf(Balance < Withdrawal, _
            DoTask1( ), _
            DoTask2( )) _
    IIf(Balance < Withdrawal, DoTask1( ), DoTask2( ))
End Sub
```

The syntax of the IIf function is:

```
IIf(true/false_clause, value_for_true, _
    value_for_false).
```

Two interesting results of the fact that IIf is a function call are that IIf can be up to 300 times slower than If, and both the second and third arguments are always evaluated.

Properties and Indexers

Both C# and VB.NET allow you to add properties to a class. Properties are functions that act as fields. You can read the value of a property or set the value of a property as if it were a storage field. The following code defines a property in C#:

```csharp
class Account
{
    int m_Balance;

    public int Balance
    {
        get
        {
            return m_Balance;
        }
```

```
      set
      {
         m_Balance = value;
      }
   }
}

class Class1
{
   static void Main()
   {
      Account Acct = new Account();
      Acct.Balance = 100;
      System.Console.WriteLine(Acct.Balance);
   }
}
```

This code shows the Account class with a Balance property, and a Class1 class that uses the property in its Main function. The Balance property declaration has a return type followed by the name of the property and no parentheses, unlike function declarations. The property has a get and a set portion. You can optionally omit the get or the set, but not both.

The set portion of the code example uses the value keyword. The line in Main that reads:

```
Acct.Balance = 100;
```

invokes the set portion of the property; the value on the right side of the equal sign, in this case 100, is stored in the value variable. value is an intrinsic keyword and must be in lowercase. The line that displays the value of the property using Acct.Balance invokes the get portion of the property.

VB also has a property construct. The C# code can be translated to VB as follows:

VB
```
Class Account
   Dim m_Balance As Integer

   Property Balance() As Integer
      Get
```

```
            return m_Balance
        End Get

        Set
            m_Balance = value
        End Set
    End Property
End Class

Module App
    Sub Main( )
        Dim Acct As Account = New Account( )
        Acct.Balance = 100
        System.Console.WriteLine(Acct.Balance)
    End Sub
End Module
```

Notice that the property declaration begins with the Property
keyword, then the name of the property followed by parentheses, and then the type of the property. In this case, the
property is of type Integer. As in C#, the Value keyword contains the value being set. In this example, when the line that
reads Acct.Balance = 100 executes, the runtime invokes the
Set portion of the Balance property. The Value variable contains the value 100.

In VB, you can omit the Set or the Get portion of the property, but not both. If you omit the Set portion, however, you
must use the ReadOnly keyword in the property declaration,
as follows:

VB
```
    Class Account
        Dim m_Balance As Integer

        ReadOnly Property Balance( ) As Integer
            Get
                Return m_Balance
            End Get
        End Property
    End Class
```

In the same way, if you omit a property's Get portion, you
must use the WriteOnly keyword, as follows:

```vb
VB   Class Account
        Dim m_Balance As Integer

        WriteOnly Property Balance() As Integer
            Set
                m_Balance = Value
            End Set
        End Property
     End Class
```

VB allows a property to accept parameters; C# does not. This feature is convenient when creating child classes that behave as arrays. For example, imagine a class called Bank that stores a series of accounts. To set the properties of an account, the developer uses the Accounts property of the class, passing as a parameter the account number, as illustrated below:

```vb
VB   Class Bank
        Private m_Accounts(100) As Account

        ReadOnly Property Accounts(ByVal AccountID _
                    As Integer) As Account
            Get
                Return m_Accounts(AccountID)
            End Get
        End Property

        Sub New()
            Dim acct As Account
            For Each acct In m_Accounts
                acct = New Account()
            Next
        End Sub
     End Class
```

The Accounts property accepts an account ID as a parameter and returns an Account from the m_Accounts array. You would use the Accounts property as follows:

```vb
VB   Module Module1
        Sub Main()
            Dim b1 As New Bank()
            Dim acct As Account = b1.Accounts(15)
        End Sub
     End Module
```

The Accounts property enables you to access a particular account within the bank's account array. However, a more elegant solution is to make it look like the Bank class itself is an array. This is done by adding an *indexer*, which is a property that accepts a parameter and is marked as the default property. You can turn the Accounts property into an indexer by adding the Default keyword to the property declaration:

```vb
Class Bank
    Private m_Accounts(100) As Account

    Default ReadOnly Property Accounts( _
    ByVal AccountID As Integer) As Account
        Get
            Return m_Accounts(AccountID)
        End Get
    End Property

    Sub New()
        Dim acct As Account
        For Each acct In m_Accounts
            acct = New Account()
        Next
    End Sub
End Class
```

When you mark the property as a default property, you can omit the name of the property when accessing a particular member of the property array:

```vb
Module Module1
    Sub Main()
        Dim b1 As New Bank()
        Dim acct As Account = b1(15)
    End Sub
End Module
```

C# also enables you to add indexers (a default property that takes parameters) to a class. The following code declares an indexer in C#:

```csharp
class Account
{
```

```
      }
   class Bank
   {
      Account[] arr = new Account[5];
      public Account this[int index]
      {
         get
         {
            return arr[index];
         }
         set
         {
            arr[index] = value;
         }
      }
   }
```

An indexer declaration looks like a property declaration, except the name of the function is this and the parameters are declared in square brackets instead of parentheses. You can write code like the following to use the indexer:

```
Bank b1 = new Bank();
b1[3] = new Account();
```

An indexer creates the illusion that the class itself works like an array. If you were to use a C# class that has an indexer in VB, you would notice that C# simply adds an Item property to the class and marks it as the Default property. Within C#, however, you cannot refer to the indexer property as Item.

The default name for the C# indexer property is Item, but you can change it using an attribute:

```
[System.Runtime.CompilerServices.IndexerName("Account")]
public Account this[int index]
{
   get
   {
      return arr[index];
   }
   set
   {
      arr[index] = value;
   }
}
```

The `IndexerName` attribute has no effect in C# client code. However, in VB.NET with this code, the Indexer property name would be Account instead of Item.

Arrays

Both languages have slightly different ways of declaring, initializing, and using arrays. Let's start with declaring arrays. In C# you use brackets after the type of the array:

[C#]
```
string[] phones;
```

It is an error to put a dimension inside the brackets; it is also illegal to put the brackets around the variable name. This code contains only the declaration for the array—phones is a reference variable that points to an object of type string[] (read: "string array").

To create an array object in C#, you do the following:

[C#]
```
//create an array of three strings
phones = new string[3];

//create an array using a variable
//to specify the dimensions
int Amount = 3;
phones = new string[Amount];
//create an array of 3 elements setting
//the array's contents at the same time
phones = new string[] {"one","two","three"};

//with the curly bracket notation you can
//even omit the call to new
string[] phones = {"1","2","3"};
```

In VB you can declare an array in several ways:

[VB]
```
'put parentheses after the type
Dim phones1 As String()
'put parentheses after the variable
Dim phones2() As String
```

You use parentheses after the data type to indicate an array. VB also lets you put parenthesis after the variable name. This syntax can be a little confusing to C# developers. In this code, phones2 is a variable of type string array—the same as phones1. It is illegal to put parentheses in both the variable name and the data type.

There are several ways of allocating an array object in VB.NET. One way is to indicate the dimensions of the array in the declaration of the array:

```VB
Dim phones1(5) As String
```

This only works if the parentheses are after the variable name—you cannot define a dimension if the parentheses are after the array type.

A crucial difference between C# and VB.NET is that in VB.NET the number inside the parentheses is really the index of the upper bound element. The above declaration produces a string array with six elements, numbered 0 through 5. In C# the numbers in brackets specify the total number of elements in the array.

It is illegal to use New when allocating an array in VB except when using the curly bracket notation (as seen in a later example). So, the following are illegal:

```VB
'this is *illegal*
Dim phones1() As String = New String(5)

'this is also *illegal*
Dim phones2() As New String(5)
```

The first statement is illegal because the compiler thinks that you are invoking a constructor for String and passing it the number 5. The second statement has several problems. The first is that you cannot use parentheses after both the variable name and the array type, and you cannot specify a dimension on the array type. The second is that you cannot use As New with array declarations.

Be careful that you do not drop the parentheses around the variable name by accident when using As New in array declarations:

```VB
Dim nums2 As New Decimal(5)
```

Of course, this line is a basic variable declaration where nums2 is a Decimal, and the value 5 is passed as the constructor's parameter. When declaring arrays, it is easy to confuse constructor invocations with array dimensions.

You do not have to use a literal number to specify the dimension of the array. The following is also valid:

```VB
Dim count As Integer = 5
Dim nums1(count) As Decimal
```

VB.NET also supports the curly bracket notation to allocate an array:

```VB
'create an array of 3 elements, setting
'the contents of the array at the same time
Dim phones1 As String()
phones1 = New String() {"one", "two", "three"}

'or you can use the curly bracket notation
'in the declaration and even omit New
Dim phones2 As String() = {"1", "2", "3"}
```

In this example, phones1 and phones2 point to arrays of strings with three elements in positions 0 to 2.

Once you allocate an array, the size of the array is immutable. In C#, if you wish to have the array variable point to an array of a different size, you must create a new array object and set the variable equal to that new array, as follows:

```C#
string[] phones = new string[5];
phones = new string[10];
```

Notice in the example that phones first points to an array of 5 elements and then points to an array of 10 elements.

VB has a Redim command that makes it a little easier to reallocate an array:

```VB
Dim phones1 As String()
ReDim phones1(9)

Dim phones2(4) As String
ReDim phones2(9)
```

In this example, phones1 is unallocated until the line that calls Redim. Redim creates an array of 10 elements and points the phones1 variable to it. In the case of phones2, however, the array is allocated once in the declaration line. Then it appears that VB is ignoring the rule that array dimensions are immutable and resizing the dimensions of the array. In actually all that VB is doing with Redim is creating a second array with the new dimensions and pointing the phones2 variable to it. The original array then becomes a candidate for garbage collection.

The use of Redim for allocating a new array is necessary because VB does not allow the use of New when working with arrays (except with the curly bracket notation).

VB has one enhancement when reallocating arrays that C# does not have: the Redim Preserve statement. With Redim Preserve, a developer can allocate a new array with new dimensions and copy all the elements from the old array to the new one in a single line of code, as follows:

VB
```
Dim nums() As String = {"5", "10", "20"}
ReDim Preserve nums(10)
```

Internally, Redim Preserve creates a brand new array. In this example, the new array has 11 elements (remember that 10 is the upper bound for the array). VB then calls a function called CopyArray in Microsoft.VisualBasic.CompilerServices. Utils. All that CopyArray does, after performing several validations for size and rank, is use the System.Array.Copy method. In fact, here is how you would do the Redim Preserve in C#:

C#
```
string[] nums = {"5", "10", "20"};
string[] temp = new string[10];
System.Array.Copy(nums,
                  0,
                  temp,
                  0,
                  nums.Length);
nums = temp;
```

Besides one-dimensional arrays, both languages let you create arrays with multiple dimensions. In both C# and VB.NET, you use a comma to indicate the rank (the number of dimensions) of the array:

C#
```
string[,] records = new string[5,5];
```

This code creates a two-dimensional array of five rows by five columns. The VB equivalent is the following:

VB
```
Dim records(4, 4) As String
'or
Dim records As String(,)
ReDim records(4, 4)
```

Both C# and VB.NET let you declare nested arrays—arrays of arrays. Each top-level element of the array points to a subarray, and each subarray can be of a different size. This type of array is called a *jagged array*. Consider the following code:

C#
```
string[][] families = new string[2][];
families[0] = new string[5];
families[1] = new string[4];

families[0][0] = "Bill";
families[0][1] = "Carole";
families[0][2] = "Bradley";
families[0][3] = "Madalyn";
families[0][4] = "Duncan";

families[1][0] = "Jose";
families[1][1] = "Laurel";
families[1][2] = "Alex";
families[1][3] = "Andy";
```

In this code, `families` is a jagged array—it is an array of string arrays. The second and third lines in the code create the subarrays. The first subarray has five elements, and the second has four. To set the elements of the array, you use the double square bracket notation, for example `families[1][0]`.

You can do the same in VB.NET, as follows:

VB
```
Dim families(1)() As String
ReDim families(0)(4)
```

```
ReDim families(1)(3)

families(0)(0) = "Bill"
families(0)(1) = "Carole"
families(0)(2) = "Bradley"
families(0)(3) = "Madalyn"
families(0)(4) = "Duncan"

families(1)(0) = "Jose"
families(1)(1) = "Laurel"
families(1)(2) = "Alex"
families(1)(3) = "Andy"
```

Notice that you use the Redim statement to set the sizes of the subarrays. To access the members of the subarrays, you use the double parentheses notation, for example, families(1)(0).

for Loops

The way in which you declare for loops in each language is different. Let's take a look at C# first:

```
for (int count=1;count < 10; count++)
{
}
```

The for statement in C# has three parts: the declaration portion, the test portion, and the action portion. Each segment is separated with semicolons.

In the declaration portion, you can literally declare anything. It could be the variable you use to keep a counter, or something totally unrelated to the loop itself. The declaration segment is also not restricted to numeric types. The following examples are valid for declarations in C#:

```
for (string count="";count != "done"; )
{
}

int m=0;
int n=0;
```

```
for (int x=0,y=0,z=0;m<10;n++)
{
}
```

Notice that in the first for declaration, the variable used is of type string. In the second for declaration, the variables in the declaration portion have nothing to do with the second and third parts of the for statement.

The second part of the for statement is the test portion. The loop continues while the test portion evaluates to true. Again, this section can have any code that results in the Boolean values true or false. In the example:

```
for (int count=1;count < 10; count++)
{
}
```

the loop ends when count is equal to or greater than 10. Because all you need in the second part of the for statement is an expression that returns true or false, the following is also a valid statement:

```
for (int count = 1,total =500;
     count < 10 && total > 200;
     count ++)
{
}
```

This for statement tests that count is less than 10 and that the total is greater than 200. If one of the two clauses returns false, the entire statement is false and the loop stops.

The last part of the for statement is the action portion. In this part of the statement, you can put a number of actions separated by commas. Traditionally you write a statement here that increases a counter. The action takes place after all the code inside the loop executes and just before the test portion is evaluated to decide if the loop should continue. The following examples show the different things you can do in the action portion of for:

```
for (int counter=1;counter < 10; counter++)
{
```

```
    int m=0;
    for (int count = 1,total =500;
        count < 10 && total > 200;
        count ++,total--,m = count *100)
    {
    }
}
```

In the inner for loop, three things occur in the action section: count is incremented by 1; total is decremented by 1;
and m is set equal to count times 100. Of course, most of the
time what you would like to write is a simple for loop that
either increases a counter or decreases a counter. Here are
two "more normal" examples:

```
string[] names = new string[100];

//navigate through the array
for (int count=0; count < names.Length;
    count++)
{
    System.Console.WriteLine(names[count]);
}

//navigate in reverse order
for (int count=names.Length; count >= 0;
    count--)
{
}
```

To write For loops in VB, you use the For, To, Next, and Step
keywords. Here is a simple example of a For loop in VB:

```
Dim count As Integer

For count = 1 To 100
Next
```

That For statement in VB has an initializing section and a test
section. The initializing section is the portion after the keyword For and before To. The variable you initialize must be
declared beforehand—VB does not let you initialize in-place.
The variable in the initialize section must be numeric. The
compiler will write IL to add 1 to this variable in each

iteration of the loop. Before entering the loop, the code evaluates the test expression after the keyword To. The test section has a value or expression to test the counter against. The loop will continue executing as long as the counter is less than or equal to this value. In the previous VB.NET example, the loop will run 100 times. Of course, this section does not have to have a literal value; for example, the following For statement uses an expression:

```vb
Dim names(100) As String
For count = 0 To names.Length - 1
    System.Console.WriteLine(count)
Next
```

In this example, count starts as 0. The loop continues until count > names.Length - 1.

You can control how the counter is incremented with the Step keyword. This example iterates through even numbers:

```vb
Dim count As Integer
For count = 0 To 100 Step 2
    System.Console.WriteLine(count)
Next
```

You can also make the counter decrement instead of increment. In that case, the To portion describes the lower limit for the counter. Here is an example:

```vb
For count = 100 To 0 Step -2
    System.Console.WriteLine(count)
Next
```

The counter begins at 100. In each iteration, the counter is decremented by 2. The loop continues until the counter is less than 0.

For/Each Loops

For/Each loops let you iterate through the members of an array or a collection such as a hash table. For a class to support for/each, it must implement the IEnumerable interface.

Both languages have mechanisms for navigating through collections that implement this interface. In C# this is done with the `foreach` command:

```
string[] names = new string[5];
foreach(string onename in names)
{
}
```

In this code, `names` is an array of strings. In the `foreach` statement, you first declare a variable compatible with the items in the array or in the collection. In this case, we declare the variable `onename` as a string. You can also declare the variable as an object, since every type is compatible with System. Object. The `foreach` loop then iterates through all the items in the collection, placing the current item in the variable you declared inside the `foreach`. Unlike VB.NET, you cannot declare the variable outside of the `foreach` loop. The following is not allowed:

```
string[] names = new string[5];
string onename;
//***this is illegal***
foreach(onename in names)
{
}
```

One limitation in C# is that the variable you declare inside `foreach` is read-only. This is also illegal:

```
//***this is also illegal***
string[] names = new string[5];
foreach(string onename in names)
{
    if (onename == null)
        onename = "John Smith";
    System.Console.WriteLine(onename);
}
```

That means that you cannot change the elements in the array.

VB also has a `For Each` construct. Unlike C#, you cannot declare the iteration variable inside `For Each`; you must declare it before using `For Each`. For example:

```
VB    Dim names(4) As String
      Dim onename As String
      For Each onename In names

      Next
```

Notice that For and Each are two separate words. In VB, the variable you use in For Each to store the current item is not read-only. Therefore, the following is legal code:

```
VB    Dim names(4) As String
      Dim onename As String
      For Each onename In names
         If onename = "" Then
            onename = "John Smith"
         End If
         System.Console.WriteLine(onename)
      Next
```

Being able to set the variable that contains the current element is of limited use. For example, in the code above, setting onename to John Smith does not change the element of the array. If you examine the array after completing the loop, you will notice that it is unaffected.

Try/Catch Blocks

Both languages can throw and catch exceptions

Try/Catch blocks are used to handle exceptions. In C# you catch exceptions in the following way:

```
C#    try
      {
         Checking check1 = new Checking();
         check1.MakeWithdrawal(1000);
      }
      catch(InsufficientFundsException e)
      {
         System.Console.WriteLine(e.ToString());
         System.Console.WriteLine(e.AccountNo);
      }
      catch
      {
         //catch everything else
      }
```

The try portion contains code that might generate an exception. In this case, if the account we are making a withdrawal from does not have enough funds, the code generates an InsufficientFundsException exception. The catch blocks tell the runtime what types of exception you wish to handle. In the example, there are two handlers: one for Insufficient-FundsException exceptions, and one for every other type of exception. It is important to order the catch blocks from more specific to more general, since only the first appropriate handler catches the exception. Therefore if the "catch all" block precedes the catch InsufficientFundsException exception block, the latter never executes. The C# compiler gives you an error if you order the catch blocks incorrectly; the VB compiler does not.

VB has a similar way of catching exceptions. Here is how you would write a similar Try/Catch block in VB:

<table>
<tr><td>VB</td><td>

```
Try
    Dim check1 As New Checking()
    check1.MakeWithdrawal(1000)
Catch e As InsufficientFundsException
    System.Console.WriteLine(e.ToString)
    System.Console.WriteLine(e.AccountNo)
Catch
    'catch everything else
End Try
```

</td></tr>
</table>

The basic differences include using an End Try statement, rather than curly braces, to indicate the end of the block. Also, in each Catch section, the variable name appears first, followed by the keyword As and the type of the exception. You do not use parentheses around the Catch variable declaration. Other than these syntax changes, in its basic form, the Try/Catch blocks in the two languages are very similar.

VB has an enhancement for catching exceptions: you can use a When clause with any Catch block. The When clause lets you specify a Boolean expression that activates or deactivates the Catch section. Look at the following code:

```VB
Try
    Dim check1 As New Checking( )
    check1.MakeWithdrawal(1000)
Catch e As InsufficientFundsException _
        When e.IsCreditAccount = False
    System.Console.WriteLine(e.ToString)
    System.Console.WriteLine(e.AccountNo)
Catch e As InsufficientFundsException _
        When e.IsCreditAccount = True
    'ignore the error, it is ok
    'to have a negative balance
Catch
    'catch everything else
End Try
```

In this Try/Catch block, the InsufficientFundsException
exception is handled differently depending on the information in the exception object. The first Catch statement, which
reports an error to the client, is executed only when the
InsufficientFundsException object's IsCreditAccount field is
False. In the second Catch statement, if the
InsufficientFundsException object's IsCreditAccount field is
True, there is no need to report the error to the client. In this
second handler, nothing visible happens—the handler
catches the exception so that the program continues.

One more thing about errors and VB. VB 1 through VB 6 used
unstructured exception handling with the On Error Resume
Next statement and its variations to trap errors. VB.NET still
supports the On Error statement. However, this is only done
for backward compatibility and is greatly discouraged.

Attribute Usage

Using attributes is an integral part of programming for the
.NET runtime. Attributes are classes that modify the behavior of other programming elements such as classes,
functions, parameters, etc. Certain programs such as compilers, the IDE, and the runtime enable you to control their
behavior by applying attributes to your code.

The way you apply attributes is somewhat different between the languages. In C#, attributes are applied using square brackets. Here is an example of defining and using an attribute in C#:

```csharp
using System;

[AttributeUsage(AttributeTargets.Class)]
public class CreditLimitAttribute : Attribute
{
    int _Max;
    int _Min;
    public int CheckStartNum=0;

    public CreditLimitAttribute(int Min,int Max)
    {
        _Min = Min;
        _Max = Max;
    }
}

[CreditLimit(1000,5000,CheckStartNum=10)]
class Checking
{
}
```

The code first declares the CreditLimit attribute, a class that is derived from System.Attribute. The constructor has two parameters, Min and Max, that report the minimum balance and maximum balance an account can have. The class also has a public field called CheckStartNum. The attribute is then applied to the Checking class.

When applying an attribute to a program element, you use brackets around the attribute. Also, you can omit the suffix on the attribute name. In this example, the class name is CreditLimitAttribute, but the compiler lets you refer to the attribute as CreditLimit. The CreditLimit attribute has two required parameters—they are the parameters of the constructor, Min and Max. After specifying the required parameters, you can also set the value of any public fields or properties in the attribute class.

In VB.NET, you can also declare and apply attributes. The main difference between the two languages is that in VB you use angle brackets instead of square brackets. Here is an example of declaring and using attributes in VB.NET:

```
VB    Imports System

      <AttributeUsage(AttributeTargets.Class)> _
      Public Class CreditLimitAttribute
      Inherits Attribute
         Dim _Max As Integer
         Dim _Min As Integer
         Public CheckStartNum As Integer

         Sub New(ByVal Min As Integer, ByVal Max As Integer)
             _Min = Min
             _Max = Max
         End Sub
      End Class

      <CreditLimit(1000, 5000, CheckStartNum:=10)> _
      Class Checking
      End Class
```

The code looks almost identical to its C# counterpart. The main differences are the use of angle brackets and the use of the := notation when setting the value of a public field or property in the attribute class.

Control Characters

Control characters are special characters that represent things in strings like carriage returns, new lines, tabs, etc. It can be very frustrating to switch languages and have to find a different way to express these characters. In C#, control characters are represented by *escape sequences*—a character or series of characters preceded by the backslash character.

VB does not use escape sequences. Instead, many control characters are represented by string constants in the Microsoft.VisualBasic.ControlChars class. The following table shows the most widely used C# escape sequences and VB ControlChars constants:

C# escape sequence	VB constant	Purpose
\n	Lf	New line
\r	Cr	Carriage return
\r\n	NewLine or CrLf	Carriage return - new line
\"	Quote	Quotation marks
\\		Backslash character
\t	Tab	Tab

Here are some examples of escape sequences:

```csharp
string s = "Hello\r\nWorld!";
System.Console.WriteLine(s);
//prints: Hello
//        World

s = "C:\\Windows\\System\\";
System.Console.WriteLine(s);
//prints: C:\Windows\System\

string sName = "Jose";
s = "SELECT * FROM ADDRESSES WHERE NAME=\""
    + sName
    + "\"";
System.Console.WriteLine(s);
//prints:
//SELECT * FROM ADDRESSES WHERE NAME="Jose"
```

Note that the backslash character, which in C# must be escaped (unless you use the @ symbol, as in @"c:\dir1\ dir2"), is represented in VB by a literal backslash character ("\"). Here are some code examples that use the Control-Chars constants:

```vbnet
Dim s As String = "Hello" & _
        ControlChars.NewLine & "World!"
System.Console.WriteLine(s)
'prints: Hello
'        World

s = "C:\Windows\System\"
System.Console.WriteLine(s)
'prints: C:\Windows\System\
```

```
Dim sName As String = "Jose"
s = "SELECT * FROM ADDRESSES WHERE NAME=" & _
ControlChars.Quote & sName & ControlChars.Quote
System.Console.WriteLine(s)
'prints:
'SELECT * FROM ADDRESSES WHERE NAME="Jose"
```

The *Microsoft.VisualBasic.DLL* assembly, which contains the
ControlChars constants, is referenced by default in Visual
Studio VB projects.

Type Comparison and Conversion

Both C# and VB.NET have a way to cast explicitly from one
type to another. Whenever the C# compiler sees that a conversion may not succeed or may result in loss of information, it issues an error. Consider the following C# code:

```
class Account
{
}

class Checking : Account
{
}

class Class1
{
    static void Main(string[] args)
    {
        Account acct = new Checking( );
        //***cannot cast implicitly***
        Checking check = acct;
    }
}
```

The compiler issues an error when you try to assign a variable of type Account to a variable of type Checking because
the compiler cannot guarantee that every Account object will
be of type Checking (you can have Savings accounts, for
example). In cases where the compiler cannot tell if the conversion will succeed, you must do an explicit cast.

In C#, an explicit cast can be done in two ways. The first is to put the type you are converting to in parentheses before the variable you are converting, as follows:

```
static void Main(string[] args)
{
    Account acct = new Checking( );
    Checking check = (Checking)acct;
}
```

This cast should succeed, since the line before the cast creates an object of type Checking. But what if the cast fails? What if the code had created an instance of the Savings class and then tried to cast Savings to Checking? When the cast fails, the runtime issues an InvalidCastExecption.

The second does not result in an exception if the cast fails. It involves using the as operator, as in the following:

```
static void Main(string[] args)
{
    Account acct = new Checking( );
    Checking check = acct as Checking;
    if (check != null)
    {
    }
}
```

When you use as to cast, the runtime returns null if the cast is unsuccessful; otherwise, the cast returns a reference to the object.

You can always test to see if an object supports a certain conversion using the is operator, as follows:

```
static void Main(string[] args)
{
    Account acct = new Checking( );
    if (acct is Checking)
    {
        Checking check = (Checking)acct;
    }
}
```

VB.NET does not warn you of possible conversions that may not succeed by default. VB has a compiler directive called `Option Strict`. When `Option Strict` is set to `Off` (its default), the compiler lets you perform any type of cast implicitly. For example:

```VB
Class Account
End Class

Class Checking
    Inherits Account
End Class

Module Module1
    Sub Main()
        Dim acct As Account = New Checking()
        Dim check As Checking = acct
    End Sub
End Module
```

This code compiles fine, even though its C# equivalent would fail. The assignment of the acct variable to a check variable would give a compiler error in C# because not every Account object is a Checking object. The compiler can warn you of conversions that may result in data loss (like a double being casted to an integer) if you turn `Option Strict` to `On`. The VB compiler then forces you to do explicit casts whenever a conversion is in doubt. The following example shows how to do an explicit cast in VB:

```VB
Option Strict On
Class Account
End Class
Class Checking
    Inherits Account
End Class
Module Module1
    Sub Main()
        Dim acct As Account = New Checking()
        Dim check As Checking = CType(acct, Checking)
    End Sub
End Module
```

Explicit conversions in VB are done with the CType function. Its first parameter is the variable you wish to cast, and the second is the type to which you wish to cast it.

VB.NET also offers a few methods as shortcuts to CType, including CLng, CStr, CBool, CChar, CInt, CObj, and CByte.

If the cast fails, whether it is explicit or implicit, the runtime issues an InvalidCastException. Before you perform an explicit cast (or an implicit cast, for that matter), it is a good idea to test whether the type can be cast to the other type. This is done with the TypeOf...Is construct. Here is an example, which tests whether the acct class can be cast to the Checking class:

```
Sub Main()
    Dim acct As Account = New Checking()
    If TypeOf acct Is Checking Then
        Dim check As Checking = CType(acct, Checking)
    End If
End Sub
```

Some FCL methods expect an instance of a System.Type object (a class that describes a particular type) as an argument. Through a Type object, you can find out such things about a class as its members, the classes in its inheritance chain, the interfaces it implements, and even any custom attributes applied to it or its members.

From an instance of a class, you can always get the class' Type object by calling the class' GetType method. Here are examples in C# and in VB:

```
class Account
{
    public void MakeDeposit()
    {
    }
}

class App
{
    static void  Main()
```

```
    {
        Account acct = new Account();
        System.Type t = acct.GetType();
        foreach (System.Reflection.MethodInfo mi
                  in t.GetMethods())
        {
            System.Console.WriteLine(mi.Name);
        }
    }
}
```

```
VB  Class Account
        Public Sub MakeDeposit()

        End Sub
    End Class

    Module Module1
        Sub Main()
            Dim acct As New Account()
            Dim t As Type = acct.GetType
            Dim mi As System.Reflection.MethodInfo
            For Each mi In t.GetMethods
                System.Console.WriteLine(mi.Name)
            Next
        End Sub
    End Module
```

Both languages also allow you to obtain a Type object for a
certain class without having to create an instance of the class
first. In C#, you can obtain the Type object for a class whose
definition is available at compile time using the typeof function, as in the following example:

```
C#  //create an array manually with the
    //array functions
    System.Array arr =
    System.Array.CreateInstance(typeof(Account),5);
```

The same thing can be done in VB with the GetType statement, as follows:

```
VB  'create an array manually with the
    'array functions
    Dim arr As Array = _
    System.Array.CreateInstance(GetType(Account), 5)
```

Object-Oriented Features

Unlike syntactic differences, which reflect merely a difference in keywords and format, *object-oriented differences* between C# and VB stem from differences in implementation between the two languages.

Inheritance Syntax

Both C# and VB can use class-based inheritance. In .NET, a class can derive from at most one other class; in other words, the system only allows single inheritance. However, a class can implement multiple interfaces. Both languages have different semantics for class inheritance and interface implementation. (Both require, though, that the inherited class be listed before any implemented interfaces.)

To use class-based inheritance in C#, list the class you would like to inherit from immediately after the derived class name, separated by a colon, as in the following example:

C#
```
class Account
{
}
class Checking : Account
{
}
```

In this example, the Checking class derives from the Account class.

Class-based inheritance in VB is done with the Inherits keyword:

VB
```
Class Account
End Class

Class Checking
    Inherits Account
End Class
```

Often, a colon is used to combine the declaration for the class with the `Inherits` statement to make the line of code look more C#-like:

```
Class Checking : Inherits Account
End Class
```

Using `Inherits` in this fashion is the same as moving the `Inherits` clause to the next line without a colon.

Method Overloading

Overloading means that several methods have the same name but different signatures. Method overloading differs slightly between the languages. Method overloading in C# and in VB.NET does not require a keyword; you simply add another method with the same name, as in the following example:

```
class Account
{
    public void MakeDeposit(int Amount)
    {
    }

    public void MakeDeposit(int Amount,
                    int AmountAvailable)
    {
    }
}
```

In this example, the Account class has two methods named MakeDeposit. The first method accepts only one integer value, and the second method accepts two integer values. The main thing to remember when overloading methods is that the compiler must know at compile time what version of the function to call. In this simple example, it is easy to see what version of the MakeDeposit method the compiler will call: it depends on the number of parameters. As you will see in a moment, it is not always easy to figure out what version will be invoked.

Method overloading in VB is done in the same fashion. The following example illustrates basic method overloading in VB:

VB
```vb
Class Account
    Sub MakeDeposit(ByVal Amount As Integer)
    End Sub

    Sub MakeDeposit(ByVal Amount As Integer, _
            ByVal AmountAvailable As Integer)
    End Sub
End Class
```

C# enables you to overload methods based on the direction of parameters. For example:

C#
```csharp
class Checking
{
    public void MakeDeposit(int Amount)
    {
    }

    public void MakeDeposit(ref int Amount)
    {
    }
}
```

The first MakeDeposit has a byval parameter, while the second has a byref parameter of the same type. This is a legal way of overloading methods in C# because, when you invoke a method that has ref parameters, you must use the ref keyword in the invocation as follows:

C#
```csharp
Checking check = new Checking( );
int Amount = 10;
//calls the version with a byval parameter
check.MakeDeposit(Amount);
//calls the version with a byref parameter
check.MakeDeposit(ref Amount);
```

In VB.NET, however, you cannot overload based on the direction of the parameters. This is because you do not have to use a keyword like ref to pass ByRef parameters to a function; how parameters are passed is defined by the method definition. Therefore, the compiler cannot distinguish between a call to a function that has a ByVal parameter and one that has a ByRef parameter of the same type.

VB.NET has an Overloads keyword that you can apply in front of overloaded method definitions, as follows:

```
Class Checking
    Overloads Sub MakeDeposit(ByVal Amount As Integer)
    End Sub

    Overloads Sub MakeDeposit(ByVal Amount As Long)
    End Sub
End Class
```

The Overloads keyword is used in front of the method declaration. However, this keyword is optional. It is required only if the class is overloading a method from a base class—if, for example, the Account class has a MakeDeposit method and Checking derives from Account and adds a second version of MakeDeposit. Overloads in a derived class tells the compiler to use hide-by-signature semantics rather than hide-by-name semantics. (See the upcoming section "Hiding Base Class Members" for a full explanation of when to use Overloads in a derived class.)

In C# it is illegal to add parameters to properties. In VB.NET, however, properties can have parameters. Therefore, it is possible to also overload properties in VB.NET. Here is an example:

```
Class Person
    ReadOnly Property Name( ) As String
        Get
        End Get
    End Property

    ReadOnly Property Name(ByVal Format As String) _
                          As String
        Get
        End Get
    End Property
End Class
```

The Person class has two definitions for the Name property: one that has no input parameters, and one that accepts a string input parameter.

Constructors and Field Initializers

Both VB.NET and C# enable the developer to add one or multiple *constructor functions*—functions that trigger automatically when the program creates an instance of the class—to a class. However, the syntax in each language is different.

To declare a constructor in C#, use the name of the class, as in the following example:

```
class Account
{
    public Account()
    {
    }

    public Account(int Amount)
    {
    }

    internal Account(int Amount, int AmountAvail)
    {
    }
}
```

This code shows the Account class with three constructors. The default constructor has no parameters. (If you do not add a constructor to your class, the C# compiler adds a default constructor automatically.) There are two other overloaded constructors. One is public and accepts one parameter, the other is marked as internal and accepts two parameters. Marking a constructor as internal means that only other classes within the same assembly may create the class while passing these two parameters.

VB also enables you to add constructors and overload constructors, and just like in C#, if you do not add a constructor, the compiler adds a default constructor automatically. In VB, constructors are declared as subroutines named New, as follows:

```
VB    Class Account
          Sub New()
          End Sub

          Sub New(ByVal Amount As Integer)
          End Sub

          Friend Sub New(ByVal Amount As Integer, _
                  ByVal AmountAvail As Integer)
          End Sub
      End Class
```

Just as in the C# example, the VB class contains three constructors. The class has a default constructor—the constructor that takes no parameters—and two overloaded constructors. One of the constructors is marked as Friend, which means that it is only visible by code in the same assembly.

Invoking Other Constructors

Sometimes it is convenient for one constructor to forward code to another constructor. When the class has multiple constructors, sometimes you may choose to write all the code in one of the constructors and simply call the master constructor from other constructors. In C#, you can call a constructor by using the this keyword, as follows:

```
C#    class Account
      {
          int m_Balance;

          public Account()
          {
              //actual code goes here
          }

          public Account(int Amount) : this()
          {
```

```
        m_Balance = Amount;
    }

}
```

Notice that the constructor definition uses a colon followed by the keyword this. The this keyword tells the compiler to write code to invoke another constructor in the class, in this case one that does not have any parameters. Another possibility is to forward the default constructor to the constructor that accepts one parameter, as follows:

C#
```csharp
class Account
{
    int m_Balance;

    public Account() : this(100)
    {
    }

    public Account(int Amount)
    {
        //actual code goes here
    }

}
```

In this case the compiler writes code so that when the default constructor is used, the first thing the function does is forward the call to the constructor that accepts one parameter.

VB also has this capability. In VB, another constructor is invoked with the Me or MyClass keyword, as follows:

VB
```vb
Class Account
    Dim m_Balance As Integer

    Sub New()
        'actual code goes here
    End Sub

    Sub New(ByVal Amount As Integer)
        Me.New()
        m_Balance = Amount
    End Sub
End Class
```

The `Me.New( )` call tells the compiler to forward the call to the constructor that takes no parameters. If you are forwarding a call to another constructor with `Me.New( )`, then the `Me.New( )` line must come before any other line in the function; otherwise, the compiler issues an error. You may also use the `MyClass` keyword, as in `MyClass.New( )`. (`MyClass` will be explained in more detail later in the section entitled "Overriding Methods.")

Invoking Base Constructors

When you derive one class from another, sometimes it is necessary to forward the child's constructor to a parent constructor. Consider the following C# example:

```csharp
class Account
{
    int m_Balance;

    public Account(int Amount)
    {
        m_Balance = Amount;
    }
}

class Checking : Account
{
}
```

With this just as it is at this point, the compiler would report an error because the Account class does not have a default constructor (a constructor that does not take parameters). When a client creates an instance of the Checking class, the runtime must invoke not only the constructor code for the Checking object, but also the constructor code for the base class, Account. It is the compiler that makes this happen. In this example, the compiler adds a default constructor to the Checking class (because the class has no constructors at the time). The first line in the constructor code that the compiler adds invokes the constructor for the base class. The latter's constructor then invokes the constructor of its base class, and so on. (If you add a constructor to your code, then the compiler adds a line to the constructor to invoke the base class constructor.) In the code above, however, the compiler is at a loss as to how to invoke the base class constructor. This is because the only constructor in the Account class accepts one parameter (and because the class has a constructor, the compiler does not add a default constructor). Thus, you have to add the code to invoke the base class's constructor yourself. The solution is the following:

```
class Checking : Account
{
    public Checking() : base(100)
    {
    }
}
```

Notice from this example that when the base class does not have a default constructor, it is necessary to add an explicit constructor to the derived class, and more importantly, to write code to invoke a base constructor. To invoke the base constructor, you must use the base keyword as if it were a function name and pass the parameters that match the particular constructor.

VB has a similar construct, except that VB uses the MyBase keyword. As in C#, if the base class does not have a default constructor, the compiler generates an error, unless you add a constructor to the derived class and invoke the base class's constructor. The following example shows the VB equivalent:

```
Class Account
    Dim m_Balance As Integer

    Sub New(ByVal Amount As Integer)
        m_Balance = Amount
    End Sub
End Class

Class Checking
    Inherits Account
    Sub New( )
        MyBase.New(100)
```

```
      End Sub
   End Class
```

Notice from this example that you must add a call to invoke the base class's constructor. To do this you must use the `MyBase` keyword. The keyword `MyBase` can be used to invoke any method in the base class. Unlike C#, in which you use the `base` keyword without specifying the name of a function, in VB you must use `MyBase` in combination with the New keyword. The VB compiler forces you to write the line `MyBase.New( )` before any other code in the constructor.

Initializers

Field initializers are class fields that are initialized in place, as in the following C# example:

```
class Account
{
   int Balance = 100;

   public void MakeDeposit( )
   {
   }
}
```

The line:

```
int Balance = 100
```

is a field initializer. This code does not have an explicit constructor function. However, if you do not provide one, the C# compiler adds a default constructor. It also adds code to this constructor to invoke the field initializers. In other words, when the code is compiled, the result should resemble the following:

```
class Account
{
   int Balance;

   public Account( )
   {
      Balance = 100; //field initializers
      base( ); //call the base constructor
```

```
        //rest of the code
    }

    public void MakeDeposit()
    {
    }
}
```

If your code contains multiple constructors, the compiler adds the code to set the field initializers to each constructor. The important thing to notice is that the C# compiler adds the initializing code to the beginning of the constructor function before calling the base constructor, and before calling any code you may have added to the constructor. The fact that the compiler adds the code for initializers before invoking the base constructor has a side effect: the this pointer in C# is not yet available at the time the field initializers are set. That means that your initializers in C# can only use constants or static fields, or invoke static (shared) functions.

In VB, things are different. VB also supports field initializers:

VB
```
Class Account
    Dim Balance As Integer = 100

    Sub MakeDeposit()
    End Sub
End Class
```

As in C#, the VB compiler adds a default constructor if one is not available. The VB compiler also adds code to each constructor to invoke the initializers. However, the order in which the initializers are invoked in relation to the base constructor is different in VB. The VB compiler turns the previous code into the following:

VB
```
Class Account
    Dim Balance As Integer

    Sub MakeDeposit()
    End Sub

    Sub New()
        MyBase.New()   'first call the base
```

```vb
                             'constructor
            Balance = 100 'field initializers go
                             'after the call to the
                             'base constructor.
               'the rest of the code goes here.
         End Sub
   End Class
```

Because the initializers are set after the call to the base constructor, by the time the field initializers are invoked, the Me object is already populated. This means that in VB.NET, it is possible to have field initializers invoke instance methods. While in C# you can only invoke Shared (static) methods, in VB there is no such limitation.

Hiding Base Class Members

What happens if a class inherits from another class and both classes have a member with the same name? If you are the author of the derived class, you may be careful not to add a member to your class that has the same name as a member in the base class. However, there is nothing stopping the author of the base class from adding a member with the same name as one of your members. Suppose you wrote a class to extend the Calculator class, and Calculator was missing a multiply method, so you added one to yours. Then, in the next release, the author of Calculator added a multiply method. Now what? Both C# and VB.NET do different things in this scenario. Let's look at how C# handles this. Consider the following code:

```csharp
class Calculator
{
   public void Add() { }
   public void Subtract() { }
   public void Multiply() { }
}

class CalculatorEx : Calculator
{
   public void Multiply() { }
}
```

CalculatorEx inherits from Calculator, and both classes have a method with the same name. If you try to compile this code, it compiles with a warning, not an error. The warning is:

```
The keyword new is required on
'CalculatorEx.Multiply()' because it hides
inherited member 'Calculator.Multiply()'
```

What the warning really means is that someone using a variable of type CalculatorEx will not be aware that there is a Multiply method in the base class. To the programmer, the only version of Multiply lives in the CalculatorEx class. However, if the programmer uses a reference to the base class type, he gets the base class version even if he creates an instance of the derived class. The following code illustrates this:

```
static void Main(string[] args)
{
    Calculator calc1 = new CalculatorEx();
    calc1.Multiply(); //calls base version

    CalculatorEx calc2 = new CalculatorEx();
    calc2.Multiply(); //calls derived version
}
```

As you can see, how you declare your variable will determine what version of Multiply is called. This behavior is called *method hiding*. There are two types of method hiding: hide-by-signature and hide-by-name. C# uses hide-by-signature. (*Signature* refers to the name of the function and its input parameters.) To illustrate the difference, imagine if Multiply in the base had different parameters from the one in the child:

```
class Calculator
{
    public void Multiply(int x, int y) { }
}

class CalculatorEx : Calculator
{
    public void Multiply(int x, int y,
                         out int result)
    {
```

```
        result = x * y;
    }
}
```

Now, it looks like the CalculatorEx class has two versions of Multiply: one that has two parameters, and one that has three parameters. It is as though the author were overloading the methods. Actually, building this code does not even generate a warning.

To complicate things, it is possible that a member in the base class is of a totally different type than the member in the derived type. For example:

```
class Calculator
{
    public bool Clear;
}
class CalculatorEx : Calculator
{
    public void Clear(int x,int y)
    {
    }
}
```

In this example, Clear is a field in Calculator and a function in CalculatorEx. In this case, CalculatorEx does not have a combination of the field and the method, since it is impossible in the same class to have two members of a different type (a field and a function, for example) with the same name. Because of hiding, a programmer using CalculatorEx only sees Clear as a method.

When hiding occurs, you can suppress the compiler warning with the new keyword. Here is an example of applying the new keyword to the previous example:

```
class Calculator
{
    public bool Clear;
}

class CalculatorEx : Calculator
{
    public new void Clear(int x,int y)
```

```
      {
      }
   }
```

The new keyword is applied to the method. This tells the compiler, "I meant to do that." Of course, new is not just for suppressing the compiler warning; it also lets you hide instead of override a method when the base method is marked as virtual (see the next section, "Overriding Methods," for details).

VB.NET lets you choose between hide-by-name and hide-by-signature semantics. First, let's take a look at how VB does hide-by-name:

```
Class Calculator
    Function Multiply(ByVal x As Integer, _
            ByVal y As Integer) As Integer
    End Function

    Function Multiply(ByVal x As Long, _
            ByVal y As Long) As Long
    End Function
End Class

Class CalculatorEx
    Inherits Calculator

    Function Multiply(ByVal x As Integer, _
            ByVal y As Integer, _
            ByVal z As Integer) As Integer
    End Function
End Class
```

This code compiles fine with only a warning. The warning reads:

```
function 'Multiply' shadows an overloadable
member declared in the base class 'Calculator'.
If you want to overload the base method, this
method must be declared 'Overloads'.
```

The Calculator class has two versions of the Multiply method, one that accepts integer values and one that accepts longs. The CalculatorEx class has a single Multiply method

---

that accepts three integer parameters. In theory, all these methods should be able to coexist in the same class. However, by default, VB uses hide-by-name semantics, which means that the programmer using CalculatorEx sees only one version of Multiply—the one in the CalculatorEx class. Any other members with the same name are hidden. This is what happens implicitly; however, VB has two keywords to control the hiding method explicitly. First, if you want to tell the compiler, "I meant to do hide-by-name" (the default), then you can use the Shadows keyword, as shown in this example:

```vb
Class Calculator
    Function Multiply(ByVal x As Integer, _
                      ByVal y As Integer) As Integer

    End Function
    Function Multiply(ByVal x As Long, _
                      ByVal y As Long) As Long

    End Function
End Class

Class CalculatorEx
    Inherits Calculator
    Shadows Function Multiply(ByVal x As Integer, _
                              ByVal y As Integer, _
                              ByVal z As Integer) _
                              As Integer

    End Function
End Class
```

With the Shadows keyword, VB uses hide-by-name semantics and suppresses the compiler warning. If you would rather have hide-by-signature semantics like C#, use the Overloads keyword. Here is the same example using the Overloads keyword:

```vb
Class Calculator
    Function Multiply(ByVal x As Integer, _
                      ByVal y As Integer) As Integer

    End Function
    Function Multiply(ByVal x As Long, _
                      ByVal y As Long) As Long
```

```
      End Function
   End Class

   Class CalculatorEx
      Inherits Calculator

      Overloads Function Multiply(ByVal x As Integer, _
                     ByVal y As Integer, _
                     ByVal z As Integer) As Integer

      End Function
   End Class
```

In this scenario, VB uses hide-by-signature semantics. Just like in C#, if the compiler can combine the definitions of the methods, it will. In this example, the programmer will see CalculatorEx as having three versions of Multiply. Using the Overloads keyword also suppresses the compiler warning.

Overriding Methods

Both C# and VB.NET have a mechanism by which you can mark a function as virtual in the base class, and then override the method in the derived class. If you create an instance of the derived class when you override a method, even code in the base class that calls the method invokes the overridden version of the method instead of the original. In C#, marking a method as virtual is done with the virtual keyword, as follows:

```
class Account
{
   public virtual void MakeDeposit(int Amount)
   {
   }
}

class Checking : Account
{
   public override void MakeDeposit(int Amount)
   {
   }
}
```

This example also shows how to override the method in the derived class by using the `override` keyword. To illustrate what it means to override a method, consider the following code:

```
Account acct = new Checking( );
acct.MakeDeposit(500);
```

In this example, a variable of type Account is used to reference an object of type Checking. Because the object is of type Checking, and because Checking overrides Account's version of MakeDeposit, the runtime invokes Checking's version of MakeDeposit even if a variable of type Account is used.

VB.NET uses `Overridable` to mark a method as virtual and `Overrides` to override the method:

```
Class Account
    Overridable Sub MakeDeposit( _
                ByVal amount As Integer)
    End Sub
End Class

Class Checking : Inherits Account
    Overrides Sub MakeDeposit(ByVal amount _
                As Integer)
    End Sub
End Class
```

As in the C# example, if a programmer assigns a variable of type Account to an object of type Checking and invokes the MakeDeposit method, the runtime invokes the Checking version of MakeDeposit.

Overriding in VB is a little more complicated when the base class has overloaded methods, and it either marks all of them or only some of them as Overridable. Consider the following example:

```
Class Account
    Overridable Sub MakeDeposit( _
                ByVal amount As Integer)
    End Sub
```

```
      Sub MakeDeposit(ByVal amount As Long)
      End Sub
End Class

Class Checking : Inherits Account
    Overrides Sub MakeDeposit(ByVal amount As Integer)
    End Sub
End Class
```

In this case, Overrides also uses the hide-by-name semantics
by default. (For a full explanation of hide-by-name, see the
previous section, "Hiding Base Class Members.") Essentially
this means that someone using a variable of type Checking
would only be able to see the MakeDeposit method in the
Checking class and not the combination of all methods from
both classes. The compiler gives you a warning when this
happens. You cannot suppress the warning and use hide-by-
name semantics by combining the Overrides keyword with
the Shadows keyword. It is illegal to combine the keywords.
However, you can choose hide-by-signature semantics
instead by using the Overloads keyword together with
Overrides in this fashion:

VB
```
Class Checking : Inherits Account
    Overloads Overrides Sub MakeDeposit( _
            ByVal amount As Integer)
    End Sub
End Class
```

If a method is marked as virtual and you override the method
in a derived class, the method continues to be virtual. This
means that another developer can inherit from your derived
class and override the method again. You can prevent the
method from being further overridden by sealing it. Sealing
in C# is done with the sealed keyword. Here is an example:

C#
```
class Account
{
    public virtual void MakeDeposit(int Amount)
    {
    }
}
```

```
class Checking : Account
{
    public override sealed void MakeDeposit(int Amount)
    {
    }
}

class SuperChecking : Checking
{
    //*** this is illegal ***
    public override void MakeDeposit(int Amount)
    {
    }
}
```

In this code, SuperChecking cannot override the MakeDeposit method further because the author of Checking marked it as sealed.

To seal a method in VB.NET you use the NotOverridable keyword:

VB
```
Class Account
    Overridable Sub MakeDeposit( _
                        ByVal amount As Integer)

    End Sub
End Class

Class Checking : Inherits Account
    NotOverridable Overrides Sub MakeDeposit( _
                    ByVal amount As Integer)
    End Sub
End Class

Class SuperChecking
    Inherits Checking
    `***this is illegal***
    Overrides Sub MakeDeposit( ByVal amount As Integer)
    End Sub
End Class
```

As in the C# example, SuperChecking is prevented from overriding the method further because the author of Checking marked the method as NotOverridable.

When you override a method, you may still want to use the code from the original method. You can invoke the original method in C# using the base keyword:

```
class Account
{
    public virtual void MakeDeposit(int Amount)
    {
    }
}

class Checking : Account
{
    public override void MakeDeposit(int Amount)
    {
        //do something before
        base.MakeDeposit(Amount);
        //do something after
    }
}
```

The Checking class overrides the MakeDeposit method, but also invokes the original method in Account using the base keyword.

VB.NET also has a way of invoking the default method in the base using the MyBase keyword:

```
Class Account
    Overridable Sub MakeDeposit( ByVal amount As Integer)
    End Sub
End Class

Class Checking
    Inherits Account
    Overrides Sub MakeDeposit(ByVal amount As Integer)
        'do something before
        MyBase.MakeDeposit(amount)
        'do something after
    End Sub
End Class
```

VB.NET has a feature for overriding methods that C# does not have. When a method is overridden, if you create an instance of the derived class, even code in the base class invokes the overridden method. However, in VB you can write code that invokes the original method using the MyClass keyword. First let's show what happens if you do not use MyClass:

```VB
Class Account

    Sub New()
        MakeDeposit(100)
    End Sub

    Overridable Sub MakeDeposit( _
                ByVal amount As Integer)

    End Sub
End Class

Class Checking
    Inherits Account
    Overrides Sub MakeDeposit( _
            ByVal amount As Integer)
    End Sub
End Class
```

In this code, if you create an instance of the Checking class, the runtime invokes the constructor for Checking first. The code does not show a constructor for Checking, so the compiler adds a default constructor, which calls the constructor in the base class. As you can see, the Account class has a constructor. The code for the constructor calls the MakeDeposit method. However, because the method is overridden, the constructor in Account ends up executing MakeDeposit in Checking, not the original version in Account. This is the default behavior in both VB.NET and C#. However, VB. NET enables you to invoke the original method using the MyClass keyword as follows:

```VB
Class Account

    Sub New()
        MyClass.MakeDeposit(100)
    End Sub

    Overridable Sub MakeDeposit( _
                ByVal amount As Integer)
```

```
    End Sub
End Class
```

In this case, the code in the constructor for Account calls the Account version of MakeDeposit. Note that `MyClass` is not the same as `Me` in VB. Using `Me` would still call the derived version instead of the original version.

Requiring/Preventing Inheritance

In C# you can mark a class as sealed. A sealed class is a class that cannot be used as a base class for another class—in other words, you cannot inherit from it. Here is an example of adding the word "sealed" to the class definition:

```csharp
class Account
{
}
sealed class Checking : Account
{
}
//***this is illegal***
class SuperChecking : Checking
{
}
```

In this code example, Account is not sealed, so Checking can inherit from it; however, Checking is a sealed class, so it is illegal for SuperChecking to inherit from it. This is not the place to have a full discussion of why you would seal, but normally you would seal a class to prevent someone from writing a subclass that overrides how you implemented an interface. Take for example the System.String class that Microsoft provides. It implements a series of critical interfaces: ICloneable, IComparable, etc. The runtime expects these interfaces to be implemented in a particular way. It would cause problems if you were to write your own string class and override the way those interfaces are implemented, and then pass instances of your string class to functions in the runtime that expected a System.String object (which you could do if you inherited from the class).

The equivalent of sealed in VB.NET is NotInheritable. Here is an example of applying this keyword to a class declaration:

```vb
Class Account
End Class

NotInheritable Class Checking
    Inherits Account
End Class

'***this is illegal ***
Class SuperChecking
    Inherits Checking
End Class
```

In this code example, Checking is free to inherit from Account; however, SuperChecking cannot inherit from Checking because it is marked as NotInheritable.

How about the opposite, a class that you must inherit from? This is done when you write a class that is not meant to be instantiated directly. For example, throughout the book I have been using Account and Checking. It could be that I decide to write Account as a base class for Checking, Savings, etc. but that my intention was for developers not to create Account directly. This is done in C# with the abstract keyword, in the following fashion:

```csharp
abstract class Account
{
}
class Checking : Account
{
}
```

Class Account is marked as abstract, which means that you cannot create instances of it directly. You can inherit from it, and then create instances of the subclass. The abstract attribute is required when one of the methods in the class is an abstract method. An abstract method is a method you must override in the derived class. Here is an example of an abstract class with an abstract method:

```csharp
abstract class Account
{
  public void ReportInfo()
  {
    System.Console.WriteLine(
    "Account is of type " + AccountType);
  }

  public abstract string AccountType { get;}
}

class Checking : Account
{
  public override string AccountType
  {
    get
    {
      return "Checking";
    }
  }
}
```

In this code example, AccountType is an abstract read-only property. That means that you must override the function and implement it in a derived class. Account provides other functionality, such as the ReportInfo function which uses the AccountType property, assuming that it has been implemented elsewhere.

The equivalent of abstract in VB.NET is MustInherit. Here is an example of a class using the MustInherit keyword:

```vbnet
MustInherit Class Account
End Class

Class Checking
    Inherits Account
End Class
```

The Account class is marked as MustInherit, which means that it is not a creatable class. You must write a class that derives from it if you want to use the functionality it provides. Normally, as in C#, this keyword is used when a member of the class is marked as MustOverride. In that case the compiler forces you to add the MustInherit keyword to the class declaration. Here is an example of the MustInherit keyword in combination with MustOverride:

```vb
MustInherit Class Account
  Sub ReportInfo( )
    System.Console.WriteLine( _
    "Account is of type" + AccountType)
  End Sub

  MustOverride ReadOnly Property AccountType( ) _
                                   As String
End Class

Class Checking
  Inherits Account

  Overrides ReadOnly Property AccountType( ) _
                                  As String
    Get
      Return "Checking"
    End Get
  End Property
End Class
```

The Account class defines a readonly property that every class author that inherits from it must override. The compiler forces you to mark that class as MustInherit.

Declaring and Implementing Interfaces

Interfaces are defined in C# and in VB.NET with the interface/Interface keyword. Here is a C# example that declares two interfaces:

```csharp
using System.Runtime.CompilerServices;
public interface IAccount
{
  void MakeDeposit(int Amount);
  int Balance { get; }
  [IndexerName("Details")]
  int this[int x]{get; set;}
}
```

```
public interface ISaveToDisk
{
    void Save();
    void Save(string Path);
}
```

As you can see, each declaration begins with the `interface`
keyword followed by the interface name. All methods in the
interface are implicitly public. Notice that the IAccount interface contains a definition for a method, a property, and an
indexer. To declare properties in an interface, you write the
property type, followed by the property name, followed by
curly brackets. If the property allows read access, you write
`get;` inside the curly brackets, and if the property allows
write access, you write `set;` inside the curly brackets. Of
course, you can combine `get;` and `set;`. You don't add a
semicolon after the closing curly bracket.

Declaring an indexer inside an interface uses a similar format as the property. The main differences are that you use
the keyword `this` for the property name, and that you have
to add at least one input parameter inside square brackets.
As with other indexer declarations, you can optionally use
the `IndexerName` attribute to set the property name for the
indexer; otherwise it defaults to Item. Refer to "Properties
and Indexers" in the "Syntax Differences" section for details
on how to declare and use indexers.

The second declaration, ISaveToDisk, shows that you can do
method overloading in interface definitions.

VB.NET has an Interface construct like C#. The VB.NET
equivalent of the above definitions is:

VB
```
Public Interface IAccount
    Sub MakeDeposit(ByVal Amount As Integer)
    ReadOnly Property Balance() As Integer
    Default Property Details(ByVal x As Integer) _
                            As Integer
End Interface

Public Interface ISaveToDisk
```

```
      Sub Save()
      Sub Save(ByVal Path As String)
   End Interface
```

VB uses `Interface/End Interface` instead of `interface` and curly brackets. The declaration of interface members is also different. The `Property` keyword is used to declare a property. By default a property has read/write access, but you can change that by adding the keywords `ReadOnly` (as you can see in the second member of IAccount) or `WriteOnly` in front of the declaration. Indexers in VB are nothing more than properties that accept parameters and are marked as default properties. In IAccount, Details is a read/write indexer. Because an indexer is a property, you can use the `ReadOnly` and `WriteOnly` keywords to restrict accessibility.

As in C# you can overload methods in interfaces, as demonstrated in the declaration of ISaveToDisk.

In both languages you can derive one interface from another. Say for example that after releasing the first version of *banking.dll*, you discover that IAccount needs an extra method, MakeWithdrawal. It is good programming practice to leave the IAccount interface alone, and declare a new interface, IAccount2, that derives from IAccount, as follows:

```
public interface IAccount2: IAccount
{
    void MakeWithdrawal();
}
```

Inheriting one interface from another is done by adding a colon at the end of the class name, followed by the name of the interface from which you wish to inherit. You can inherit from more than one interface—you just separate the interfaces with commas, as in the following:

```
public interface IAccount2: IAccount,
                            ISaveToDisk
{
    void MakeWithdrawal();
}
```

Inheriting one interface from another can also be done in VB.NET using the Inherits keyword:

```
VB    Interface IAccount2
          Inherits IAccount
          Sub MakeWithdrawal( )
      End Interface
```

To inherit from multiple interfaces, you can either add two Inherits statements or list all the interfaces in a single Inherits statement, separated by commas. Here is an example of inheriting from multiple interfaces:

```
VB    'you can put both interface names
      'in the same Inherits line
      Interface IAccount2
          Inherits IAccount, ISaveToDisk
          Sub MakeWithdrawal( )
      End Interface

      'or write a different Inherits line for
      'each interface
      Interface IAccount2
          Inherits IAccount
          Inherits ISaveToDisk
          Sub MakeWithdrawal( )
      End Interface
```

Let's talk about how to implement interfaces in each language. In C# you first tell the compiler that your class intends to implement the interface. This is done in the same way that you specify class-based inheritance: using the colon followed by the interface name:

```
C#    class Checking : IAccount
```

You can derive a class from multiple interfaces, but remember that you can only inherit from one concrete class. In the inheritance line you would list the non-interface class first, then the interfaces separated by commas.

The next step is to implement the methods. The simplest way to do this in C# is to add a public method with the same name as the interface's method and with the same signature. Here is an example:

```csharp
interface IAccount
{
   void MakeDeposit(int Amount);
}

class AccountImpl : IAccount
{
   public void MakeDeposit(int Amount)
   {
   }
}
```

As you can see from the example, AccountImpl inherits from
the interface. It has a public MakeDeposit method with a
name that matches the interface's method name and has a
matching signature (the parameters are of the same type).
When the compiler sees a public method with the same
name and signature as the interface method, it uses the
method as the implementation of the interface method. Suppose there were two interfaces with the same method name
as in the following:

```csharp
interface ISaveToDisk
{
   void Save();
}

interface IWhales
{
   void Save();
}

class Checking : ISaveToDisk, IWhales
{
   public void Save()
   {
   }
}
```

In this example, both ISaveToDisk and IWhales have a Save
method with the same signature. If I derive my class from
both interfaces and add a Save method with the same signature to my class, then the Save method becomes the implementation method for both Save interface methods. This

could be good or bad; good because it saves on typing, bad because it assumes that I want the same implementation for both methods. This syntax has another side effect. For this syntax to work, the method must be marked public—anything other than public results in a compiler error saying that the interface method has not been implemented. Making the method public means that there are two ways to reach that method. One is through a variable of the implementing class' type, and one is through a variable of the interface type. Here is an example:

```csharp
interface IAccount
{
    void MakeDeposit(int Amount);
}

class Checking : IAccount
{
    public void MakeDeposit(int Amount)
    {
    }
}

class App
{
    static void Main(string[] args)
    {
        Checking check = new Checking();
        check.MakeDeposit(500);
        IAccount acct = new Checking();
        acct.MakeDeposit(500);
    }
}
```

As you can see in Main, you can call the MakeDeposit method either through a variable of type Checking or through a variable of type IAccount. However, this has the side effect that the implementation method is accessible outside of the assembly. You can block access to the method through the variable of the class' type and you can map two interface methods with the same name to two different implementations with another syntax C# provides for implementing methods. This other syntax involves making the

implementation method's name equal to the name of the
interface, plus a dot, plus the name of the interface method.
Here is the example that defines two interfaces with the same
name revisited:

```C#
interface IAccount
{
   void MakeDeposit(int Amount);
}

interface ISaveToDisk
{
   void Save();
}

interface IWhales
{
   void Save();
}

class Checking : ISaveToDisk,IWhales
{
   void ISaveToDisk.Save()
   {
   }
   void IWhales.Save()
   {
   }
}
```

With this syntax, the implementation methods are private.
The only way to reach them is through the interface. And you
are not allowed to put an access modifier keyword such as
public (or even private) in one of these methods. To invoke
the methods in this fashion you would do the following:

```C#
ISaveToDisk sav = new Checking();
sav.Save();
```

You can always reach the method through the interface even
if the method is private in scope.

VB.NET uses a different approach for implementing interface methods. First of all, to tell the compiler that you are

going to support an interface, you use the `Implements` keyword as follows:

```vb
Class AccountImpl
    Implements IAccount
End Class
```

You can list more than one interface in the same `Implements` statement by separating each interface name with a comma. Or, you can add multiple `Implements` statements. Just like in C#, you can inherit from at most one non-interface class, but you can implement more than one interface. If you do inherit from a non-interface class, you must put the `Inherits` statement before any `Implements` statements.

To implement an interface method in VB, you add a method with any name; it does not have to be the same name as the interface method name. However, you must match the signature to the interface method (the number of parameters, and types of parameters). Then you write `Implements` and the method you are implementing at the end of the method declaration, as illustrated in the next example:

```vb
Class AccountImpl
    Implements IAccount

    Sub MakeDeposit(ByVal Amount As Integer) _
            Implements IAccount.MakeDeposit

    End Sub
End Class

'or you can also use a different method name
'as long as you match the method signature
Class AccountImpl
    Implements IAccount

    Sub MyMethod(ByVal Amount As Integer) _
            Implements IAccount.MakeDeposit
    End Sub
End Class
```

The important thing is to match the signature of the method and add the `Implements` section at the end of the method declaration.

All methods in VB are public by default. In the previous example, if you examine the second AccountImpl class, you'll see that there are two ways to invoke the implementation method. One is through a variable of type AccountImpl and one is through a variable of type IAccount, as shown below:

```VB
Interface IAccount
    Sub MakeDeposit(ByVal Amount As Integer)
End Interface

Class AccountImpl
    Implements IAccount

    Sub MyMethod(ByVal Amount As Integer) _
            Implements IAccount.MakeDeposit
    End Sub
End Class

Module Module1
    Sub Main()
        Dim acct As New AccountImpl()
        acct.MyMethod(500)
        Dim iacct As IAccount = New AccountImpl()
        iacct.MakeDeposit(500)
    End Sub
End Module
```

Notice that you can reach the method through a variable of the class type. However, when invoking the method, you use the name you gave the implementation method. In our example the name was MyMethod. On the other hand, if you use the interface, then you refer to the method by the interface's method name (MakeDeposit in our example).

You can restrict how developers access this method through variables of the class type by adding an access modifier to the implementation method. For example, you could mark the method private, as in the following example:

```VB
Class AccountImpl
    Implements IAccount

    Private Sub MyMethod(ByVal Amount As Integer) _
        Implements IAccount.MakeDeposit
    End Sub
End Class
```

With the above definition there is only one way to reach the method now: through an interface variable.

The VB syntax also enables you to map two interface methods to the same implementation. Consider the following example:

```VB
Interface ISaveToDisk
 Sub Save()
End Interface

Interface ISaveToNetwork
 Sub Save()
End Interface

Class Checking
 Implements ISaveToDisk, ISaveToNetwork

 Sub SaveToAnything() _
        Implements ISaveToDisk.Save, _
        ISaveToNetwork.Save
 End Sub
End Class
```

As the code shows, you can list more than one interface method in the Implements portion of the declaration.

Suppose a class implements an interface. For the sake of argument, let's say class AccountImpl implements the IAccount interface. Then suppose that class Checking inherits from AccountImpl. By inheriting from AccountImpl, Checking automatically gains support for the AccountImpl interface. That is a good thing, but suppose that Checking would like to have a different implementation for one of the methods in AccountImpl. Both languages enable you to override an interface implementation from a base class; however, this is done differently in each language.

In C#, if you use the method of adding public functions to implement the interface, you can override by marking the implementation method as virtual:

```C#
interface IAccount
{
    void MakeDeposit(int Amount);
}

class AccountImpl : IAccount
{
    public virtual void MakeDeposit(int Amount)
    {
    }
}

class Checking : AccountImpl
{
    public override void MakeDeposit(int Amount)
    {
    }
}
```

The code example above defines an interface called IAccount. It then implements the interface in AccountImpl. Checking derives from AccountImpl, so it gains full support for the interface. However, if Checking decided that it needs different functionality for MakeDeposit, one way to override the method is for the author of AccountImpl to mark the method as virtual. Then the developer of the Checking class can override the implementation.

Suppose that the author of the base class does not want to mark the method as virtual. Then, as the author of the derived class, you can reimplement the interface. This is done by adding the interface again to the inheritance list, as follows:

```C#
class AccountImpl : IAccount
{
    public void MakeDeposit(int Amount)
    {
    }
}
```

```
class Checking : AccountImpl, IAccount
{
   public void MakeDeposit(int Amount)
   {
   }
}
```

It will not work correctly if you do not reimplement the interface; calling the method through the interface will call the base class's implementation. Note also that when you reimplement the interface, you do not have to reimplement every method in the interface.

This technique of reimplementing the interface should also be used if you implement the interface in the base class using private methods. The following example illustrates this:

C#
```
class AccountImpl : IAccount
{
   void IAccount.MakeDeposit(int Amount)
   {
   }
}

class Checking : AccountImpl, IAccount
{
   void IAccount.MakeDeposit(int Amount)
   {
   }
}
```

In VB you cannot reimplement an interface in the derived type. This means that the only way to override the implementation of an interface in a derived class is to mark the implementation method in the base class as Overridable and then override the method in the derived type. The following example illustrates how to do that:

VB
```
Interface IAccount
   Sub MakeDeposit(ByVal Amount As Integer)
End Interface

Class AccountImpl
   Implements IAccount
```

```vb
    Public Overridable Sub MakeDeposit( _
        ByVal Amount As Integer) _
        Implements IAccount.MakeDeposit
    End Sub
End Class

Class Checking
    Inherits AccountImpl

    Public Overrides Sub MakeDeposit( _
            ByVal amount As Integer)
    End Sub
End Class
```

This technique makes it possible to have a different implementation for MakeDeposit in the Checking class. If you were to define a parameter of type IAccount, set it equal to an object of type Checking, and then call the MakeDeposit method, the runtime would execute the Checking version of MakeDeposit. The only problem with this approach is that it requires a developer to mark the base class method as Overridable.

A big part of interface-based programming is finding out whether a particular object supports a certain interface. In C# this is done in two ways. One way is to use the as operator. The as operator performs a safe cast. If the class does not implement the interface then the as operator returns null; otherwise it returns a reference to the interface you requested. This example uses the as operator:

```csharp
static void SaveAccount(IAccount acct)
{
    ISaveToDisk sav = acct as ISaveToDisk;
    if (sav != null)
        sav.Save();
}
```

This function receives an object that supports the IAccount interface. The code then asks the object if it supports the ISaveToDisk interface using the as operator. If it does, it returns a reference to the interface. If it doesn't, it returns null.

You can also find out in C# if an object supports a particular interface with the is operator. The is operator returns true if the object supports the interface and false if it does not. This example uses the is operator:

```csharp
static void SaveAccount(IAccount acct)
{
    if (acct is ISaveToDisk)
    {
        ISaveToDisk sav = (ISaveToDisk) acct;
        sav.Save();
    }
}
```

In this example, the code finds out first if the object acct supports the ISaveToDisk interface. If it does, the is test returns true. Then, the code performs an explicit cast to the ISaveToDisk interface, which is done by putting the type you want to convert to in parentheses in front of the variable.

Incidentally, if we were to cast to an interface that the object does not support, the runtime would return an InvalidCastException exception. Here is an example of how to catch that exception:

```csharp
static void SaveAccount(IAccount acct)
{
    try
    {
        ISaveToDisk sav = (ISaveToDisk) acct;
    }
    catch (System.InvalidCastException ex)
    {
    }
}
```

Another way to test whether an object supports the interface is to attempt to cast the object to the particular interface and trap for the exception. This method is not very efficient because exceptions are performance expensive and should be avoided if possible.

In VB.NET you test whether an object supports an interface using the TypeOf/Is keywords. Here is an example of testing for an interface in VB:

```vb
Sub SaveAccont(ByVal acct As IAccount)

  If TypeOf acct Is ISaveToDisk Then
    Dim sav As ISaveToDisk = CType(acct, ISaveToDisk)
    sav.Save( )
  End If
End Sub
```

The code tests whether the particular object supports the ISaveToDisk interface first. If it does, TypeOf/Is returns true. Next, the code does an explicit cast to the interface by using the CType function. CType is required if Option Strict is turned on for the project. Otherwise, in VB you would be able to do an implicit cast, in the following fashion:

```vb
Option Strict Off
Dim sav As ISaveToDisk = acct

Option Strict On
Dim sav As ISaveToDisk = CType(acct, ISaveToDisk)
```

Either way, if the cast were to fail, the runtime would generate an InvalidCastException exception. To protect against it, you could put the cast statement inside a Try/Catch block:

```vb
Sub SaveAccont(ByVal acct As IAccount)
  Try
    Dim sav As ISaveToDisk = CType(acct, ISaveToDisk)
    sav.Save( )
  Catch ex As System.InvalidCastException
  End Try
End Sub
```

Of course, it is more efficient to test for the interface with TypeOf/Is than to blindly cast and trap any error.

Delegates and Events

Delegates are classes that store a reference to a method in another class. A delegate describes the prototype for a

---

function or a subroutine. You can declare a variable of a certain type of delegate and point the variable to a method in a class. Then you can invoke the method using that variable.

Delegates are used for setting up callback functions. In a callback, the client code invokes a method on the server component to perform a task, and passes as a parameter a reference to a function in its own class. The server class holds on to this reference and, when it is done executing the task, invokes the method in the client class to notify it that it is done performing the task. Sometimes callback functions are used to report the progress of a certain function. The server class invokes a method in the client class periodically as it is performing a task for the client to report on the status of the task and sometimes to enable the client to cancel the task.

To declare a delegate in C#, you use the `delegate` keyword as follows:

```
delegate bool ReportProgress(string msg);
```

The above definition could be placed inside or outside a class. It defines a delegate type named ReportProgress. The ReportProgress type can store references to functions that take one parameter of type string and return a Boolean value. You can define the delegate to have any type of input and output parameters.

You can declare a delegate in the same fashion in VB.NET using the `Delegate` keyword:

```
Delegate Function ReportProgress( _
        ByVal msg As String) As Boolean
```

In this case the ReportProgress version will store functions that accept a string parameter and return a Boolean.

Once you declare a delegate prototype, you can declare variables of that delegate type and assign them to functions that match the prototype. The following example shows how to declare a variable of the delegate type and assign it to a function in C#:

```csharp
delegate bool ReportProgress(string msg);

class MailClient
{
    public bool PrintToScreen(string msg)
    {
        System.Console.WriteLine(msg);
        return true;
    }
}

class Class1
{
    static void Main(string[] args)
    {
        MailClient mc = new MailClient();
        //using the delegate
        ReportProgress rg =
        new ReportProgress(mc.PrintToScreen);
    }
}
```

The PrintToScreen method of the MailClient class has the same signature as the delegate prototype (accepts one string parameter, returns a Boolean). Therefore, you can declare a variable of type ReportProgress and make the variable point to the PrintToScreen function. This is illustrated in the Main function of Class1. As you can see, you simply declare a variable of type ReportProgress and set it equal to a new ReportProgress, passing the function name as the parameter for the constructor. The constructor for the delegate accepts a function as input (a function that takes a string parameter and returns a Boolean in this case).

In VB.NET you can use a syntax similar to C#; however, the language also provides some shortcuts. Here are some examples in VB.NET of declaring and initializing delegates:

```vbnet
Delegate Function ReportProgress(ByVal _
                msg As String) As Boolean

Class MailClient
    Public Function PrintToScreen( _
            ByVal msg As String) As Boolean
```

```
        System.Console.WriteLine(msg)
        Return True
    End Function
End Class

Module Module1
    Sub Main( )
        Dim mc As New MailClient( )

        'assigning a delegate through
        'the constructor
        Dim rg1 As New ReportProgress( _
                AddressOf mc.PrintToScreen)
        'assigning a delegate through the
        'equals sign
        Dim rg2 As ReportProgress = _
                AddressOf mc.PrintToScreen
    End Sub
End Module
```

VB.NET uses the AddressOf operator to assign the function
to the delegate. Also, VB enables you to create a delegate
simply by setting the delegate variable equal to the address of
a function.

Using a delegate is done in the same way in both languages:
simply use the variable name followed by the parameters. In
C# this is done as follows:

C#
```
    bool Cancel = rg("Connecting...");
```

And in VB.NET this is done as follows:

VB
```
    Dim Cancel As Boolean = rg1("Connecting...")
```

Both languages support events, and in both languages events
are based on delegates. An event in essence is a field inside a
class that maintains a list of delegates. When you fire an
event, the runtime invokes each delegate in the list. When
you declare an event in your class, the compiler changes the
declaration to a field and two methods: one to add a delegate to the list and one to remove the delegate from the list.

In C# you have to first declare a delegate to declare an event.
Here is an example:

```
delegate bool ReportProgress(string msg);
class MailServer
{
    public event ReportProgress OnReportProgress;

    public void Send()
    {
        bool Cancel = OnReportProgress("Sending...");
    }
}
```

The example shows how to declare an event and how to invoke the event. To declare an event you must declare a delegate prototype first. Then you use the event keyword, followed by the delegate type, followed by the name of the event. To trigger the event, you use the name of the event followed by the delegate's parameters.

In VB.NET, declaring an event can be done in two ways. One way is to use the C# style, in which you define a delegate first, and then you declare an event of that type of delegate. The other way is to declare both the delegate and the event at the same time. The following example shows how to declare an event using both mechanisms:

```
Delegate Sub ReportProgress( ByVal msg As String)

Class MailServer
    Event OnReportProgress As ReportProgress
    Event OnSendBegin()
    Event OnSendEnd(ByVal LastMsg As String)

    Public Sub Send()
        RaiseEvent OnSendBegin()
        RaiseEvent _
            OnReportProgress("connecting...")
        RaiseEvent OnSendEnd("Done!")
    End Sub
End Class
```

In this example, OnReportProgress is declared as an event of type ReportProgress. ReportProgress is a delegate. One difference between C# and VB.NET, however, is that VB.NET does not allow you to have events that return values.

Therefore, the ReportProgress delegate is marked as a Sub instead of a Function. Interestingly, VB lets you handle an event from a C# class that returns a value; you just can't declare an event that returns a value in VB.

The same class defines two other events, OnSendBegin and OnSendEnd. Both are declared in-place without having to declare a delegate first. The VB compiler then silently creates delegate types for you using the prototype of the event definition.

The last example also shows how to fire an event. In VB this is done with the RaiseEvent keyword. You cannot call the event function directly.

In C#, a class wanting to receive event notifications does so in the following fashion:

```
class MailClient
{
    public bool PrintToScreen(string msg)
    {
        System.Console.WriteLine(msg);
        return true;
    }

    public void Compose( )
    {
        MailServer ms = new MailServer( );
        ms.OnReportProgress +=
        new ReportProgress(PrintToScreen);
    }
}
```

The MailClient class wants to receive OnReportProgress events from the MailServer class. In order to do so, the class needs to have a function that has the same signature as the delegate prototype for the event. Then you refer to the class's event as if it were a field (class name dot event name), and use the += operator to register for event notifications. To unregister, you can use the -= operator. To the right of +=, you create a new instance of the delegate class that was used to declare the event and pass to the constructor the name of the function you wish to use to catch the event notification.

In VB.NET you use a slightly different approach:

```VB
Class MailClient
    Dim WithEvents ms As MailServer

    Public Sub PrintToScreen( ByVal msg As String) _
    Handles ms.OnReportProgress
        System.Console.WriteLine(msg)
    End Sub

    Sub Compose( )
        ms = New MailServer( )
    End Sub
End Class
```

The first step in requesting event notifications is to declare a member variable of the class that provides the event. MailServer has an OnReportProgress event; therefore, you declare a variable of type MailServer. However, you must use the WithEvents keyword in the declaration to receive event notifications. The second step is to declare a method that has the same signature as the event. In the declaration of the method, you add a Handles clause plus the variable name you declared with WithEvents, a dot, and the name of the event. In the example, the clause reads:

```VB
Handles ms.OnReportProgress
```

The last step is to register for notifications. This is done by setting the WithEvents variable to an instance of the class that fires the event. To unregister from notifications, you set the WithEvents variable equal to Nothing, as follows:

```VB
Sub Silent
    ms = Nothing
End Sub
```

Comparing Classes

Classes fall under two main categories: value types and reference types. Value types are classes that are derived from

---

System.ValueType. They include primitive types like integer, long, double, decimal, bool or Boolean, etc., structures, and enumerated types. Reference types are all other classes. They include classes that are derived directly or indirectly from System.Object. The String class is actually a reference type that in some ways behaves like a value type.

One difference between value and reference types is the way in which their memory is allocated and deallocated. Another difference is the way in which the compiler interprets comparisons of type members.

To test two objects for equality in C#, you can use the == operator (two equals signs). For example:

```
class RefPerson
{
    int Age;
    string Name;

    public RefPerson(string Name, int Age)
    {
        this.Name = Name;
        this.Age = Age;
    }
}

class Class1
{
    static void Main(string[] args)
    {
        RefPerson pr1 = new RefPerson("Jose",12);
        RefPerson pr2 = new RefPerson("Jose",12);

        if (pr1 == pr2)
            System.Console.WriteLine("Equal");
    }
}
```

This code example defines the RefPerson class. RefPerson is a reference type—it inherits from System.Object directly. The class has two fields, Age and Name. It also has a single constructor that requires a name and an age to be passed in as arguments. The class Class1 has a Main procedure that creates two instances of the RefPerson class, both of which have the same values for name (Jose) and age (12). The crucial part of the example is the comparison using the == operator. It turns out that with the above definition of the class, the C# compiler translates == to an identity check rather than an equality check. An *identity check* only takes into consideration where the objects live in memory. In other words, "Is pr1 pointing to the same memory location as pr2?" This would be true only if pr1 and pr2 point to the same object. In this case, because the code creates two instances of the Ref-Person class, that can never be true.

The equivalent of == in VB is the = operator. However, in VB there is no way to compare two reference objects using the = operator. To compare for identity (two variables pointing to the same object), you must use the Is operator. Thus, this C# code can be translated to VB as follows:

```vb
Class RefPerson
    Dim Age As Integer
    Dim Name As String

    Sub New(ByVal Name As String,  ByVal Age As Integer)
        Me.Name = Name
        Me.Age = Age
    End Sub
End Class

Class Class1
    Shared Sub Main()
        Dim pr1 As New RefPerson("Jose",12)
        Dim pr2 As New RefPerson("Jose",12)

        If pr1 Is pr2 Then
            System.Console.WriteLine("Equal")
        End If
    End Sub
End Class
```

The Is operator in VB is used to test identity. Just like in the C# example above, the code will not report that pr1 Is pr2 is true, since both variables point to unique objects.

The .NET runtime provides a way to test for equality instead of identity. Equality is a test based on the values of the fields in the class and not on the location of the objects in memory. The System.Object class provides a function called Equals for this purpose. By default, this function does not do anything useful. It is up to the developer to override this function so that it does something meaningful. Normally, a developer would write something like this:

```vb
Class RefPerson
    Dim Age As Integer
    Dim Name As String

    Sub New(ByVal Name As String, _
            ByVal Age As Integer)
        Me.Name = Name
        Me.Age = Age
    End Sub

    Overrides Overloads Function Equals(ByVal other _
                                    As Object) As Boolean
        If Me.Name = other.Name And _
        Me.Age = other.Age Then
            Return True
        Else
            Return False
        End If
    End Function

    Overrides Function GetHashCode() As Integer
        Return Name.GetHashCode() * Age.GetHashCode()
    End Function
End Class
```

As you can see, this code overrides two methods, Equals and GetHashCode. (For reasons beyond the scope of this book, you should also override GetHashCode whenever you override the Equals function.) The Equals function is defined in this case so that for two instances of the RefPerson class to be equivalent, both instances' name and age must be the same. To test for equality in both languages, you can just call the Equals method directly. For example:

```vb
If p1.Equals(p2) Then
```

or:

```
if (p1.Equals(p2))
```

C#, however, has another way of testing for equality instead of identity using the == operator. The author of the class to be compared can override the == operator in the class. Here is an example:

```
class RefPerson
{
    int Age;
    string Name;

    public RefPerson(string Name, int Age)
    {
        this.Name = Name;
        this.Age = Age;
    }

    public static bool operator ==(
    RefPerson p1,RefPerson p2)
    {
        if (p1.Name == p2.Name && p1.Age==p2.Age)
            return true;
        else
            return false;
    }

    public static bool operator !=(
    RefPerson p1,RefPerson p2)
    {
        if (p1 == p2)
            return false;
        else
            return true;
    }
}
```

The RefPerson class now has two other functions. These functions use a technique available only to C#: operator overloading. Here, the == (equal) operator and the != (not equal) operator are overloaded. If you override the == operator, the compiler forces you to override the != operator. In fact, you should also override the Equals and the GetHashCode

---

methods then, since == and Equals should perform the same
test if you are providing an override for the operator. If you
override the == operator, when the compiler sees code that
tests the two objects, instead of performing an identity test,
the compiler calls the overloaded function. Consider once
again the following code that tests the two references:

```
class Class1
{
    static void Main(string[] args)
    {
    RefPerson pr1 = new RefPerson("Jose",12);
    RefPerson pr2 = new RefPerson("Jose",12);

    if (pr1 == pr2)
        System.Console.WriteLine("Equal");
    }
}
```

This code is identical to that in the previous example. In that
example, == tested for identity. If you override the == operator in the RefPerson class, however, the same code now tests
for equality.

Inside the IL

Operator overloading is purely a compiler trick and only
works within C# programs. When you override the equals
operator (and of course the not equals operator), the compiler adds two functions to your class: op_Equality and op_
Inequality. Then the compiler watches for code that uses the
operator. Whenever it sees such code, instead of checking for
identity, it simply calls the op_Equality function in the class.

Unfortunately, VB does not support operator overloading.
What's more, if a VB program uses a C# class that overloads
an operator, using the operator will not have any effect.
From the VB side, the overloading of == looks like the

developer added a function called op_Equality to the class. Interestingly, you can call op_Equality and all other functions resulting from operator overloading from VB. By default, IntelliSense does not display them in the list of methods for the class, but you can have IntelliSense include them by selecting Tools → Options from the main menu, then selecting Text Editor → Basic → General from the list of properties, and unchecking the "Hide advanced members" option. This option is checked for VB projects by default and unchecked for C# projects by default (another difference between the two languages).

The only way to test for equality in VB.NET is to use the Equals function from System.Object.

Thus far, all the examples in this section have focused on comparing reference types. Comparing value types is very different. For one thing, C# will not let you use the == operator with two non-primitive value types. If you define a structure, for example, C# will not let you use the == operator to compare two instances unless you overload the == operator in the value type. Consider the following code:

```
struct ValPerson
{
    int Age;
    string Name;

    public ValPerson(string Name, int Age)
    {
        this.Name = Name;
        this.Age = Age;
    }
}

class Class1
{
    static void Main(string[] args)
    {
        ValPerson pv1 = new ValPerson("Jose",12);
        ValPerson pv2 = new ValPerson("Jose",12);

        if (pv1 == pv2)
```

```
        System.Console.WriteLine("Equal");
    }
}
```

This code results in a compiler error because the ValPerson
structure (which the compiler turns into a class derived from
System.ValueType) does not have an implementation for the
== operator. If you were to add one just like in the RefPerson
class example above, then the code would compile fine.

VB does not enable you to compare two non-primitive value
types using the = operator. Since there is no way to override
the = operator (or any other operator) in VB, the only way to
test for the equality of two structures is to override the
Equals operator in the class, as shown earlier.

String Comparisons

Strings are a strange entity. They are reference types; they are
not derived from System.ValueType, so they follow the same
rules of memory allocation and deallocation as other reference types. On the other hand, developers like to use strings
as if they were value types. For example, it is very handy to
be able to do the following:

```
string sName1 = "Jose";
string sName2 = "Jose";

if (sName1 == sName2)
    System.Console.WriteLine("Equal");
string sName3 = sName1 + sName2;
```

Here, the string class acts as a value type in three ways. The
first is the string assignment. Although the string class is a
reference type, it is possible to create an instance of the class
by simply declaring a variable of the type and assigning it a
value. Thus the lines:

```
string sName1 = "Jose";
```

and:

```
string sName2 = "Jose";
```

allocate two instances of the string class.

The second is in the if statement. When comparing two strings, you want to compare the contents of the string, not whether the two variables are pointing to the same object in memory. If the string object were a reference type without value type properties, we would not be able to test string contents with code like:

```
if (sName == "Jose")
```

The third is that you can concatenate two strings with the plus sign.

VB also lets you treat the string type as a value type. In fact, the code above can easily be translated to VB:

```
Dim sName1 As String = "Jose"
Dim sName2 As String = "Jose"

If sName1 = sName2 Then
    System.Console.WriteLine("Equal")
End If
```

Internally, however, the two languages work differently. In C#, using the == operator with string objects causes the compiler to call op_Equality for the string class. You will recall from the previous example that op_Equality is the function the compiler adds when you override the == operator in a class. The .NET team responsible for the system classes chose to override this operator in the string class. Internally, op_Equality makes a call to the Equals function in System. String. The Equals function always performs a case-sensitive comparison between the strings. Thus, in C#, "Jose" is never equal to "jose".

In VB, when you compare two strings using the = operator, the compiler changes the code to a call to a helper function in *Microsoft.VisualBasic.dll*. This function essentially does one of two things: a case-sensitive comparison, or a case-insensitive comparison. The decision is based on the Option Compare compiler directive specified at the top of the code files. If you specify Option Compare Text at the top of the code file, then all comparisons between strings are case-insensitive. If you specify `Option Compare Binary` (or omit the directive), then the equal signs uses a case-sensitive comparison. This principle is illustrated below:

```VB
Option Compare Binary
Dim s1 As String = "A"
Dim s2 As String = "a"

'these two strings should not be equal
'because of the casing
If s1 = s2 Then
    System.Console.WriteLine("Equal")
End If
```

```VB
Option Compare Text
Dim s1 As String = "A"
Dim s2 As String = "a"

'strings are equal because comparison
'is case insensitive
If s1 = s2 Then
    System.Console.WriteLine("Equal")
End If
```

IDE Differences

This section concerns primarily differences in the way that Visual Studio configures projects in C# and VB. These differences in turn often affect the operation of each language's compiler.

AssemblyInfo.x

Whenever you generate a new project, each language adds either an *AssemblyInfo.vb* (for VB) or an *AssemblyInfo.cs* file (for C#). This file contains attributes for the assembly. Think of the assembly as the project. Assembly attributes are things like Title, Description, Version Number, etc. for the resulting EXE or DLL. Each language puts slightly different attributes in each file. The following code list shows each C# attribute, followed by the VB.NET equivalent:

```
[assembly: AssemblyTitle("")] //C#
<Assembly: AssemblyTitle("")> 'VB

[assembly: AssemblyDescription("")] //C#
<Assembly: AssemblyDescription("")> 'VB

[assembly: AssemblyConfiguration("")] //C#
'VB .NET does not add this attribute

[assembly: AssemblyCompany("")] //C#
<Assembly: AssemblyCompany("")> 'VB

[assembly: AssemblyProduct("")] //C#
<Assembly: AssemblyProduct("")> 'VB

[assembly: AssemblyCopyright("")] //C#
<Assembly: AssemblyCopyright("")> 'VB

[assembly: AssemblyTrademark("")] //C#
<Assembly: AssemblyTrademark("")> 'VB

[assembly: AssemblyCulture("")]  //C#
'VB does not add this attribute

//C# does not add this attribute
<Assembly:CLSCompliant(True)> 'VB

//C# does not add this attribute
<Assembly: Guid("xxxxxxxx-xxxx-xxxx-xxxx-xxxxxxxxxxxx")>
'VB

[assembly: AssemblyVersion("1.0.*")] //C#
<Assembly: AssemblyVersion("1.0.*")> 'VB

[assembly: AssemblyDelaySign(false)] //C#
'VB does not add this attribute

[assembly: AssemblyKeyFile("")] //C#
'VB does not add this attribute

[assembly: AssemblyKeyName("")] //C#
'VB does not add this attribute
```

Let's discuss the attributes that are not added by default in both languages.

The `System.Reflection.AssemblyConfiguration` attribute in C# projects enables you to specify the target for the project, such as Debug, Release, or any custom target you declare. Targets are known in .NET as configurations. However, this attribute has little impact on the program. It is only useful if a program using reflection (functions to read a program's metadata) specifically looks for it. In other words, someone has to write custom logic to search for the attribute for the attribute to be meaningful.

`System.Reflection.AssemblyCulture` (in C# projects) is one of the pieces of information that the assembly resolver uses when locating an assembly in your system. The assembly resolver locates assemblies based on the assembly's name, the assembly's version, the assembly's culture, and the assembly's originator. It seems that the culture would therefore be an important attribute to include. However, the culture attribute should only be applied to satellite DLLs. *Satellite DLLs* are DLLs that have no executable code; they only have resources for strings, icons, etc. Supposing an application needs to display a localized message box, the application could load a particular satellite DLL based on the culture. If your program has executable code, then you must leave this attribute blank; otherwise, the compiler returns an error. The compiler will mark any DLL or EXE with executable IL (and therefore with the `AssemblyCulture` attribute set to blank) to `Culture=neutral`.

The `System.Runtime.InteropServices.Guid` attribute (added to VB.NET projects) is used for COM interop. Every type library (a type library describes the interfaces and classes your .NET assembly makes available to COM projects) has a GUID that identifies it, called a LIBID. This attribute lets you set the LIBID when you create a COM type library from your .NET assembly. The .NET Framework SDK ships with a tool called *tlbexp.exe*. This tool can read a .NET assembly's metadata and generate a COM type library from it. Then you can use the type library in VB 6 or in Visual C++ 6.0 with the `#import` directive.

Whenever you compile a .NET project, the IDE automatically generates one of these LIBIDs, so even if you do not have this attribute in your project, your type library will have a LIBID. However, unless you set this attribute explicitly, every time you compile you run the risk of the compiler generating a new number. Having a new GUID every time you recompile is not desirable. The GUID itself is generated using an algorithm that takes into consideration the name of the assembly and the names of all the public classes and interfaces, as well as the project's version number. Project GUIDs are *not* guaranteed to be unique. If two people in two different machines generate the same types of projects with the same names for each class and interface, and assign the same version number, they will both end up with the same LIBID. Adding this attribute means that you are taking full control of when that GUID gets changed.

The `AssemblyDelaySign`, `AssemblyKeyFile`, and `AssemblyKeyName` attributes (added to C# projects) have to do with digitally signing your assembly. Before adding an assembly to the global assembly cache (which contains assemblies that are shared among multiple projects), the assembly must be digitally signed. These attributes influence how the assembly is signed. Typically, these attributes should be added to projects whose resulting DLL will be added to the GAC. If you need to digitally sign an assembly, you must add these attributes to your source code (in VB by hand). An alternative to adding these attributes to your code is to compile your program with the command-line compiler and use the /delaysign, /keyfile, and /keycontainer switches.

Default/Root Namespace

A *namespace* is a prefix that is added to each class name in order to make the name of the class unique. Many times, companies use the company name plus the project name as a namespace name.

Both VB.NET and C# enable you to specify a default namespace through a project setting. To get to this setting in VB.NET, first locate the Solution Explorer window, right-click on the project name, and choose Properties from the popup menu. A dialog appears with project settings; under Common Properties → General, you will see a field called Root namespace. Follow the same steps in C#, but the field in the Common Properties → General dialog is called Default namespace.

In C#, having a default namespace means that any time you ask the IDE to add a new class file to your project, the wizard creates a file that declares the default namespace, then adds the new class definition within the namespace. For example, if your default namespace is WidgetsUSA, when you choose Project → Add Class from the menu, the wizard creates a source file that looks like the following:

```
namespace WidgetsUSA
{
    public class Class2
    {
    }
}
```

If you change the default namespace setting, then any new files you generate will have the new namespace name; old files retain the previous namespace name. You could also set this property to blank, and then the wizard would not add a namespace declaration.

In VB.NET, when you assign a root namespace to your project, all classes in the project automatically become part of the root namespace. The wizard does not add a namespace definition to the source files; the setting takes effect at compile time. If you add a namespace declaration to the source explicitly, the compiler still appends the root namespace to the name of each class. If you set the root namespace to WidgetsUSA and write code that defines a Banking namespace with a class called Account, as follows:

```
VB    Namespace Banking
          Class Account
          End Class
      End Namespace
```

the full name of the Account class will be WidgetsUSA.Bank-ing.Account. The root namespace will always be added to every class as a prefix. By default, VB sets the root namespace property to the project name. Because the setting only takes effect at compile time, if you change it in the middle of development, then the namespace is changed for every class. You can also leave the root namespace field blank.

Startup Object

Project Properties → Common Properties → General has a setting called Startup Object. Both C# and VB.NET have the same setting in the same location. In C#, you can set this to either (Not set), the default value, or to the name of a class with a static Main procedure. If you set this option to (Not set) then the compiler will look for one class that has a static Main procedure. If you have more than one class with a static Main, you can't leave the setting as (Not set); you must set it to a specific class or the compiler will complain.

VB.NET has an option that reads Sub Main. This option is equivalent to (Not set) in C#. If you select this option, the compiler looks for a class or a module with a Sub Main. If you have two classes with Sub Main, the compiler complains. You then have to pick a specific class from the drop-down list.

A significant difference between the two languages concerns the handling of the startup form in a WinForms project. C# adds the following code to the first WinForm the wizard creates:

```
C#    static void Main()
      {
         Application.Run(new Form1());
      }
```

Since the form is a class, the `static void Main` procedure satisfies the Startup Object requirement. If you add another form with the wizard, the second form will not have a static Main method. If you want the second form to be the startup form, then you have to cut and paste the code from the first form into the second form. VB.NET takes a different approach. The wizard does not add any startup code, and you can set the Startup Object to any form class. Then, when you compile, VB will add startup code at the IL level to the form you selected as the Startup Object. In fact, the IL code looks like the C# code above.

App.ico

Both languages enable you to add a custom icon for the application. The icon setting in C# is under Project Properties → Common Properties → General → Application icon; in VB, it is under Project Properties → Common Properties → Build → Application icon. C# lets you customize the default icon. When you generate a C# project, the wizard adds a file called *App.ico* with the default icon to the project files and changes the Application icon setting to point to this file. In VB.NET this setting is set to (Default icon) by default. There's no icon file that you can edit if you leave this set to the default.

Imports/using

As you may have seen in the "Syntax Differences" section, both languages enable you to omit the namespace name of a class by using the `Imports/using` statement. The IDE offers an extra feature for VB projects. VB projects enable you to add `Imports` statements that apply to all files in the project through Project Properties → Common Properties → Imports.

COM References

Both languages enable you to add references to COM components. You do that by right-clicking on the References line in the Solution Explorer window and choosing Add Reference from the popup menu. You will then see the Add Reference dialog. From there, you can click on the COM tab and select a COM class. When you do so, the IDE creates a .NET Interop DLL (a wrapper assembly) that describes the interfaces and classes in the COM DLL. The IDE then copies the Interop DLL to the output directory of the application referencing it. Whenever you make a call through a .NET wrapper class, the call is forwarded to the COM class.

C# goes a step further by having two properties in the IDE, under Project Properties → Common Properties → General, that enable you to digitally sign the resulting .NET DLL. They are Wrapper Assembly Key File and Wrapper Assembly Key File Name. Why would you want to digitally sign the DLL? Because to share the DLL among different executables, it is best to add the DLL to the Global Assembly Cache (GAC), and to add it to the GAC you must digitally sign the DLL. Thus if you generate a public/private pair key file, you can specify the name of the file in the Wrapper Assembly Key File setting and Visual Studio .NET will automatically use that file to digitally sign the resulting DLL.

VB projects do not have such a setting. To do the same thing in a VB project, you must create the Interop DLL by hand using a tool called *tlbimp.exe* that ships with the .NET Framework SDK (it should be already installed in your system if you installed Visual Studio .NET). *tlbimp.exe* has a command-line switch called /keyfile that lets you specify a public/private pair key file to use to digitally sign the Interop DLL. Once you generate the DLL with *tlbimp.exe*, you then add a regular .NET Reference to your project instead of a COM Reference.

Compiler Constants

Both C# and VB.NET support selected compiler constants. You can define compiler constants by adding a command to your source code or by adding the constants to your project settings through the IDE. The following table shows the different commands you use to define and test for compiler constants:

VB	C#	Description

#Const	#define	Defines the constant within code. For example:
		`#Const TestNumber=45`
		or
		`#define Production`
		In C# you cannot set the constant to value. It is either defined or undefined.

#If…Then	#if	Tests for the constant. If the result is true, the code following the #if is compiled; otherwise, the code is omitted.
#Else	#else	Compile alternate code.
#ElseIf	#elif	Add a second condition.
N/A	#undef	Undefine a constant. For example: `#undef TestNumber`

The following code fragments show the use of the compiler directives in each language:

VB
```
Sub ReadProgramSettings()
#If DEBUG Then
    #Const SettingsFile = _
           "C:\Code\Config\Settings.txt"
    ReadSettingsFromTextFile()
#Else
    ReadSettingsFromDatabase()
#End If
End Sub

#If DEBUG Then
    Sub ReadSettingsFromTextFile()
        'code to read settings from
        'SettingsFile
```

```
      End Sub
   #Else
      Sub ReadSettingsFromDatabase()
      End Sub
   #End If
```

How does that differ from a regular If statement? The #If is evaluated at compile time rather than at runtime. Only the code within the block that meets the criteria will be compiled.

The compiler constant DEBUG is defined through a setting in the IDE: Project Properties → Configuration Properties → Define DEBUG constant. If DEBUG is defined, the resulting VB code will be:

VB
```
   Sub ReadProgramSettings()
      #Const SettingsFile = _
            "C:\Code\Config\Settings.txt"
      ReadSettingsFromTextFile()
   End Sub

   Sub ReadSettingsFromTextFile()
      'code to read settings from
      'SettingsFile
   End Sub
```

Otherwise, the code would look like the following:

VB
```
   Sub ReadProgramSettings()
      ReadSettingsFromDatabase()
   End Sub

   Sub ReadSettingsFromDatabase()
   End Sub
```

The C# equivalent code is the following:

C#
```
   void ReadProgramSettings()
   {
   #if DEBUG
      ReadSettingsFromTextFile();
   #else
      ReadSettingsFromDatabase();
   #endif
```

```
   }

#if DEBUG
   void ReadSettingsFromTextFile()
   {
      //code to read settings from
      //SettingsFile
   }
#else
   void ReadSettingsFromDatabase()
   {
   }
#endif
```

One of the biggest differences between the two languages is that in VB compiler constants must have values. Also the VB #If statement lets you write a full conditional statement. You could do the following, for example:

[VB]
```
#If OutputFile = "C:\Windows\File.txt" _
    And Trace=True Then
```

In C# constants are either defined or undefined, and they can't be compared to literal values. In C#, you simply write:

[C#]
```
#define VAR
#if VAR
```

without assigning VAR a value.

Option Explicit, Option Strict, Option Compare

Probably one of the biggest differences between C# and VB.NET when it comes to project settings is that VB has three unique properties: Option Explicit, Option Strict, and Option Compare. You can find these properties in Project Properties → Common Properties → Build. Option Explicit controls whether variable declaration is required. If set to Off, you can use a variable without first declaring it. The type of such a variable will be System.Object. I can almost see some C# developers' jaws drop in disbelief—what kind of language is VB that it lets you use variables without declaring them first? To be honest, most experienced VB developers always set this option to On, and it is now (actually for the first time in VB's history) set to On by default. There is no equivalent in C# for this feature.

The second setting is Option Strict. This is a new setting for VB developers. If you set Option Strict to Off, you do not need to assign a type to your variables. In other words, it is perfectly legal to write code that says:

```
Dim Acct = New CChecking()
```

In that case, Acct will be of type System.Object. This feature has two other side effects. One is that with Option Strict On, the compiler will issue a compile-time error if it detects a narrowing conversion or if it cannot guarantee that the conversion will succeed. The developer can fix the error by using an explicit cast. In VB explicit casts are done with the *CType* function or an equivalent. (See "Type Comparison and Conversion" in the "Syntax Differences" section for a full explanation.) The only reason this option should be set to off is to use late binding (see "Late Binding (VB)" in the "Unique Language Features" section for details).

The third option in VB.NET, Option Compare, was explained in detail in the "String Comparisons" section.

Errors and Warnings

Both compilers generate errors (of course), and both generate warnings as well, but the C# compiler can generate different types of warnings. Warnings come in different levels, 0 through 4. Warning level 0 means that no warnings are reported. Warning level 1 means that only severe warnings are reported.

VB.NET projects let you set the warning level to either 0 or 1. This is controlled through Project Properties → Configuration Properties → Build → Enable build warnings (checked by default). C# lets you set the warning level through Project Properties → Configuration Properties → Build → Warning

Level. A warning level of 2 means that the compiler also displays warnings that have to do with method hiding. Warning level 3 also warns about expressions that are always true or always false. Warning level 4 (the default) displays informational warnings.

Unique Language Features

This section covers features that are specific to each language. Throughout the book I have been pointing out things that are in one language and not in the other if the other language at least has a feature that remotely resembles that of the first. This section covers things in each language that are not really available in the other.

Unsafe Blocks (C#)

Perhaps the biggest difference between C# and VB.NET is that C# enables developers to write blocks of unsafe code. Unsafe blocks (or unmanaged blocks) are mainly used to access API functions or COM functions that require pointers and enable C# developers to manipulate memory directly through pointers. In C#, it is illegal to use pointers unless the code is inside an unsafe block.

Most of the time, C# developers will not use unsafe blocks, since unsafe code can't be verified and therefore requires much higher security rights than code that can be verified to be safe. The following shows an example of unsafe code:

```
class Class1
{
    static unsafe void Main(string[] args)
    {
        //who says strings cannot be changed
        string sName = "Joseph Mojica";

        fixed (char *Temp = sName)
        {
            char *ch = Temp;
```

```
            ch += 4;
            *ch = (char)0;
            ch += 1;
            *ch = (char)0;
        }

        System.Console.WriteLine(sName);
    }
}
```

This code accesses the buffer of a string variable directly and changes two characters. Normally, strings are immutable, but with unsafe code, you can manipulate memory directly. Notice that the function needs to be marked as unsafe. Also notice the use of the fixed keyword. fixed pins a variable to a certain location of memory so that if garbage collection occurs, the collector will not move the contents of memory that the variable points to to another location.

using (C#)

Because .NET reclaims memory using garbage collection, an object may not be released for a while, even if there are no variables pointing to it. Sometimes, however, it is good to deallocate expensive resources right away rather than waiting for the garbage collector. A good example of this is an ADO.NET Connection object, which potentially keeps a handle to a SQL Server connection. Connections are expensive resources and should be reclaimed as soon as possible. For that reason, the .NET framework defines the IDisposable interface. You can ask an object if it supports IDisposable, then call the interface's Dispose method. In the implementation of Dispose, the author of the object with the expensive resource should release the resource. A good programming practice is to write code that uses objects with expensive resources inside a try...finally block, and in the finally section of the block to add code to ask for IDisposable and call Dispose. This is done so that if by some chance there is an exception in the code, the finally block will always take care of calling Dispose.

C# has a construct called using that writes this code automatically; it generates IL to enclose the code for an object inside a try...finally block, and to call the Dispose method on the object before exiting the block of code. Let's see first what the code would look like without the using function in both C# and VB.NET. Then we will see what it looks like with the using function.

```
void OpenDatabase( )
{
  string cstr =
      "Provider=Microsoft.Jet.OLEDB.4.0;";
  cstr += "Data Source=c:\\csvqs.mdb;";
  OleDbConnection conn = new
                    OleDbConnection(cstr);
  try
  {
    conn.Open( );
    //do something useful here
  }
  finally
  {
    IDisposable disp = conn
                      as IDisposable;
    if (disp!=null) disp.Dispose( );
  }
}
```

This code opens a connection to an Access database and then is supposed to do something useful with the connection. If something goes wrong, however, or if the code exits normally, the code within the finally block will ensure that the Dispose method is called. The same is possible in VB.NET with the following:

```
Sub OpenDatabase( )
  Dim connstr As String
  connstr = "Provider=Microsoft.Jet.OLEDB.4.0;"
  connstr &= "Data Source=c:\\csvqs.mdb;"
  Dim conn As New OleDbConnection(connstr)
  Try
    conn.Open( )
    'do something useful here
  Finally
```

```vb
      Dim disp As IDisposable
      If TypeOf conn Is IDisposable Then
          disp = conn
          disp.Dispose()
      End If
   End Try
End Sub
```

Again, just as in C#, the Dispose code is inside a Finally block so that it always executes. Now let's see how this is more easily done in C# with the using command:

```csharp
void OpenDatabase()
{
  string cstr;
  cstr = "Provider=Microsoft.Jet.OLEDB.4.0;";
  cstr += "Data Source=c:\\csvqs.mdb;";
  using (OleDbConnection conn =
        new OleDbConnection(cstr))
  {
    conn.Open();
  }
}
```

With using, you can either declare a variable inside the using statement or use an existing variable. Before the code exits the using block, it will call the Dispose method on the object. The only way to do this in VB is to write the try...finally block by hand.

Documentation Comments (C#)

C# supports documentation comments, which are enhanced comments. They use three slashes (///) instead of two as the comment symbol and also use various XML tags. (The complete list of XML tags is in the Visual Studio .NET documentation under "Tags for Documentation Comments.") The compiler then searches through the code for those special comments and turns them into XML or even HTML documentation. Let's see some sample code:

```csharp
/// <summary>
/// Adds a certain amount of money
/// to the account's balance.
```

```
/// </summary>
/// <param name="Amount">The Amount
/// parameter contains the amount to
/// deposit.</param>
/// <returns>Total balance</returns>
public int MakeDeposit(int Amount)
{
    _Balance+=Amount;
    return _Balance;
}
```

The function is MakeDeposit. The documentation comments are found above the function. The code uses three tags: <summary> to describe the function, <param> to describe a parameter, and <returns> to describe the return parameter. One nice feature in VS .NET is that you can write the function first, then type /// above the function declaration. VS .NET then automatically writes the skeleton of the documentation tags with a <summary> tag, a <param> tag for each parameter, and a <returns> tag.

You then have to turn on the XML documentation feature for your project. You do that by specifying an output filename for the documentation in Project Properties → Configuration Properties → Build → XML Documentation File. If you name the XML Documentation File the same as your assembly and put it in the same directory as the assembly, the comments will appear in Intellisense when you reference the assembly.

Interestingly, if you turn on XML Documentation, the compiler will issue warnings for any public class that does not have XML Documentation information.

Operator Overloading (C#)

There is a feature in C# called *operator overloading*, which enables you to redefine operators (such as the plus operator) for a class. In other words, you can redefine what it means to add two instances of your class. There are a number of unary and binary operators you can override. (For a complete list of operators see "C# Operators" in the Visual Studio .NET documentation.)

When you overload operators, you always add a `public static` function followed by the type it returns (normally the same type as the class for which you are writing the overloaded operator function), followed by the `operator` keyword and the operator you are overloading.

For the following examples, assume that the functions are inside a class called Checking. The following code overloads the ++ unary operator:

```
public static Checking operator ++
                (Checking source)
{
   source._Balance++;
   return source;
}
```

A unary operator accepts one parameter of the type of the class for which the overloaded function belongs. In this example, we redefine the ++ operator to mean "add one to the balance of the account."

Here is an example of overloading a binary operator:

```
public static Checking operator +
                (Checking source, int Amount)
{
   source._Balance += Amount;
   return source;
}
```

Binary operators require two parameters, one for the type for which the operator overloading function is written, while the second can usually be of any type. This example defines what happens when you add an integer to a Checking object. The function adds the integer to the overall balance. In fact, here is some code that shows how one would use the + operator in the class:

```
private void Form1_Load(object sender, System.EventArgs e)
{
```

```
        Checking check = new Checking();
        check+=100;
    }
```

This code creates an instance of the Checking class, then adds 100 to the object. Adding 100 causes the code for the + operator to trigger.

There is no way to overload operators in VB.

Inside the IL

When you overload operators, the C# compiler renames the function to op_thenameofoperator. For example:

```
public static class Checking  op_Increment(class
Checking source)
public static class Checking  op_Addition(class
Checking source, int32 Amount)
```

If a developer writes code that uses the operator, like Check++, the compiler changes that code into a method call to one of the op_something functions, in this case op_Increment. If you use another language, like VB, that doesn't recognize operator overloading, the overloaded operator function appears like any other function, but with the name op_something. In fact, you can call the operator overloaded functions from VB using the op_something name.

Late Binding (VB)

One of the biggest features that VB has that C# does not have is late binding. In the COM days, late binding meant using the IDispatch interface for an object. In .NET, late binding has nothing to do with IDispatch, but involves using the .NET reflection functions. With reflection, a developer can inspect an object at runtime and find out all the methods the object supports as well as the parameters required to make the calls. Reflection is not just for making method calls; it enables the developer to find out almost anything about a class: fields, methods, properties, events, constructors, etc.

Both languages enable you to use the reflection functions directly. Here is an example in C# that invokes the MakeDeposit method in the Checking class:

```
public class Checking
{
    int _Balance;

    public void MakeDeposit(int Amount)
    {
        _Balance += Amount;
    }
}

class App
{
    static void Main(string[] args)
    {
        Checking check = new Checking( );
        Type t = typeof(Checking);
        System.Reflection.MethodInfo mi =
                t.GetMethod("MakeDeposit");
        object[] pars = new Object[] {100};
        mi.Invoke(check,pars);
    }
}
```

In this code, we first obtain a Type object. The Type object is the entry point to the reflection information. We then call the Type object's GetMethod function to retrieve a MethodInfo object containing information on the Checking class' MakeDeposit method. This is simplified by the fact that the Checking class has only one MakeDeposit method; if it had overloaded versions of MakeDeposit, we would have to tell it which overloaded version we wanted. Once you retrieve a MethodInfo object, you can call its Invoke method, passing an instance of the object and an array of objects with the values for the parameters of the function to be invoked. Invoke then makes the actual method call.

You can convert this code to VB. However, unlike C#, VB offers a mechanism for using reflection without using the reflection functions; it is called late binding. Take a look at the following code:

```vb
Option Strict Off
Dim check As Object = New Checking()
check.MakeDeposit(100)
```

For this to work, you must turn off Option Strict. Then you declare a variable of type Object and assign it to any object or structure. You can then write code that invokes any public method in the object or structure, passing any number of parameters. The compiler turns that code into a call to one of the VB helper functions that uses reflection to make the actual method call.